Michael Sadler once wrote a doctoral thesis on the failure of the French Symbolist poets to write fiction. He has since managed marginally better himself. His work includes writing for BBC Radio 3 and television, a history of music and rock in strip cartoons, a French art-house film starring Jean-Louis Trintignant and translations of Marivaux and Musset for the BBC/RSC. In 2002–3 he adapted Terry Johnson's *Hysteria* for John Malkovich's production at the Théâtre Marigny in Paris, and is in the process of translating Tom Stoppard's new play. He was recently made a Knight of the National French Tripe Fraternity, is the ex-president of the Livarot cheese festival and a regular contributor to the Canal+ programme *Le Cercle*. He is a Senior Lecturer at the London University Institute in Paris, where he runs an MA course in Contemporary French Studies. He likes Schubert, Led Zeppelin and, if he ever had the chance to taste it, Château Pétrus. He lives in Paris and the Touraine, where he grows his own leeks. He has a French wife, a French-English daughter, and was recently awarded the Légion d'honneur.

Also by Michael Sadler

An Englishman in Paris
An Englishman à la Campagne

An Englishman
Amoureux

Love in Deepest France

Michael Sadler

POCKET
BOOKS

London • New York • Sydney • Toronto

First published in Great Britain by
Simon & Schuster UK Ltd, 2007
This edition first published by Pocket Books, 2008
An imprint of Simon & Schuster UK Ltd
A CBS COMPANY

1 3 5 7 9 10 8 6 4 2

Simon & Schuster UK Ltd
Africa House
64–78 Kingsway
London WC2B 6AH

www.simonsays.co.uk

Simon & Schuster Australia
Sydney

A CIP catalogue record for this book is
available from the British Library.

ISBN: 978-1-41652-243-0

Typeset by Rowland Phototypesetting Ltd
Bury St Edmunds, Suffolk
Printed and bound in Great Britain by
Cox & Wyman Ltd, Reading, Berks

To Lulu and to Daisy

1

Et ça recommence . . .

Would I never crack the mystery of France?

As the red Mazda drove through the village of Toison, where the moustached ladies with their orange crash helmets seemed forever to await the Davigel frozen food lorry, my heart beat faster. When I turned up the drive of cherry trees and stopped in front of the long, low house with its red tiled roofs and its heart-shaped peepholes cut into the crumbling oak of the shutters, I was over the moon. The cows of my neighbour Aimé Matou were grazing in the adjacent field. Normally laid back – *ce sont des vaches très cools* – the herd expressed its excitement at my return with a sympathetic fanfare of liquid pats. From the bottom of the garden the leeks, cruelly abandoned during the trip to England, undulated like a chorus of lascivious hula-hula girls, and, high on the dose of organic guano I had slipped them, waved their fronds:

'*Coo coo!*' they called. *Maï-quel!* Look how we've grown!'

The smell of the house hit me as soon as I opened the door: a mixture of wax polish and woodfire, a hint of *lardons*, a shimmer of *andouillette* – in all a heady mixture of Marcel Proust and pork. A moment of bliss with a slug of a tart, tender Vouvray, a sliver of pig's ear bought especially for the occasion, a chunk of baguette and a tomato from the garden. Heaven.

Once again, I surrendered to the embrace of France.

In my wallet, slipped lovingly between my Super-U fidelity card and details of my blood group if ever *boudin* should get the better of me, was a photograph of Lou Charpin, the new woman of my life, the muse of Pont de Ruan*, *ma Française à moi*. It was for her that I had returned. She must share this moment with me. The snap was dog-eared by passion. I pinned it to the main beam – a glimpse of Lou fishing by the sea in a white linen dress, with her mass of black hair, her skin tanned by the August sun, her smile which would melt the knees of a garden gnome. I was but a shrimp in her net.

She was attracted by *mon look British*? So be it. *Ainsi soit-il*. My shoes needed attention. Not for me those garish airbags which now pass for footwear. No, sir. My feet – or my *nougats* as Henri the roof carpenter would have it – only feel at ease encased in fine, time-worn leather.

My brogues in a plastic bag, I left for Loches. Towns have souls: there are sulky towns, frowning towns, sharp-tongued towns, quick-tempered towns and carefree towns. Loches, blonde, sedate, demure, with her peeking towers and stone lacework, is *une ville coquette*.

The Mail Drouin is a lime-tree walk under the walls of the old town. I parked the Mazda in the shade – it was red enough as it was – and wended my way to the shop of Monsieur Michel. Cobblers in Britain are of two sorts: either hunchbacked dwarves straight out of Norwegian folk tales, or recently reformed glue-sniffing

---

* See *An Englishman à la Campagne* (Simon & Schuster, 2004)

hooligans on remand. Monsieur Michel with his pink cheeks and his apron looked more like a Gilbert and Sullivan innkeeper. His shop was attractively chaotic – shelves piled high with re-soled shoes in neatly labelled brown paper parcels, endless stands for bootlaces, a machine for cutting keys, another for engraving door plates – *Annette Giraud, District Nurse* in Gothic lettering – huge shoe-horns for riding boots, and the vast humming locomotive behind him with its spinning black brushes, its grindstones and knives.

Monsieur Michel surveyed the heels. He could read shoes as others the dregs of coffee cups. In Touraine you find two kinds of wear. Vouvray wears away the prow, Chinon, the stern. I'd been a little heavy on red. He asked me to come back in half an hour.

Nothing is more delightful than shopping in Loches when you have nothing to buy. You spot some warm *rillons* – cubes of long-simmered belly of pork – just the thing for tea. A kilo of *pêches de vigne* – wild peaches ripened on age-old stunted trees that grow in the vines, a pig's ear to replace the one just nibbled . . . You never know, an unexpected visitor, a glass of wine – 'You wouldn't by any chance have an ear to nibble?'

In a half-hour I was back at Monsieur Michel's, tottering under the weight of my shopping. My shoes were ready, re-heeled, and with them he gave me an attractive plastic shoe-horn with the inscription *Les Chaussures en Fête à la Cordonnerie Michel*. I made my way back to the car, the weight of the plastic bags cutting canyons in my fingers.

Jusque là tout baigne. So far so good.

I left the car park, turned right into the rue Balzac, and was about to turn left again at the Auberge du Mail with its very tempting 12 Euros menu – *salade de gésiers* (gizzard salad, like many things, sounds a shade less attractive once translated), *entrecôte béarnaise, dessert* and a small carafe of wine. But half past three was a little late for lunch and a little early for dinner. *Dommage*. A pity. A beige Citroën BX was approaching me, the driver, sporting a tartan cap complete with pompom, a clone of Monsieur Dumas the ace mechanic and apéritif wizard of Toison. I was about to wave a friendly hand when the driver, peering through the windscreen, suddenly lifted his finger at me.

Surely I had not seen what I had seen? A lifted finger? No, no. Quite inconceivable. Not in Loches, an attractive sub-prefecture of the Indre et Loire, altitude 72 metres, on a happy-go-lucky summer afternoon.

Ready explanations leaped to mind. It was a trick of the light. Or some deep-seated, long-inhibited fear had erupted from the dark pit of the Id. The local paper *La Nouvelle République* was doubtless to blame. The pages were full of stories of road rage: *Bernard Goudron, a retired butcher of 72, destroyed the wing of a Renault 14 belonging to Claude Deguay, a retired ironmonger, with a pickaxe.*

I drove on towards *Lots-Lots*, one of the highlights of the Loches shopping scene. *Lots-Lots* specializes in bankrupt stock. If you are looking for something essential i.e. a 1996 guide to fish restaurants in the Paris suburbs, a box of car deodorants in the form of golf balls, then *Lots-Lots* is the place for you. The red light behind Atac turned green and I crossed towards the elegant building of the Palais de Justice. A Peugeot 306 drove down from the Rex cinema. From a distance the driver looked like Eric Moineau, the supercharged electrician. I was about to wave a cheery hand when, once again, he also raised his finger.

This time it certainly wasn't a mirage.

French gestures I had by now, for the most part, sorted out. I even practised them in front of the bathroom mirror. You tug on the lower lid of the left eye to indicate you are not to be taken for a ride. *Mon œil* means, 'pull the other one.' To express shock or admiration, you wave your right hand up and down at waist-level as if you'd burned it on the hot plate all the while saying *'Oh la la.'* You stroke your right cheek (of the face, I hasten to add) with the outside of the right hand to indicate boredom as you languorously utter, *'La barbe* – beard.' This will doubtless seem extravagant to a nation parsimonious with their extremities, nevermind take it as gospel.

But the raised finger!

I had innocently returned to the charming provincial town of Loches in order to get myself re-heeled. Why should I be exposed to such aggression? Was it because the Mazda had British plates? We have, it is true, been long at daggers drawn. Loches counts amongst its distinguished past visitors Joan of Arc who, according to the French, is the only continental dish the British have ever succeeded in cooking correctly. Was her spirit still abroad? Was the desire to boot the intruder into the sea still on the agenda?

Conciliatory by nature, it was my instinct to turn the other cheek. But escape was impossible. The Queen was sitting next to me in the passenger seat of the Mazda, wearing her seat belt and a large turquoise hat.

'Do something, Michael. For heaven's sake, man, don't be such a cretin. *Ne soyez pas couillon!*'

'Of course, Your Majesty. Right away.'

A Peugeot 606 appeared on the starboard bow. The driver's hand left the wheel and he began to lift his finger, like some discourteous chipolata. Before he could complete the gesture, I was down on him like a ton of bricks. I gave him a well-rehearsed rendition of the Honorary Arm *(le bras d'honneur)* – the right hand slaps the inner elbow of the left arm, causing the lower section to move skywards. The Gallic equivalent of 'Up yours.' *Messieurs les Anglais, tirez les premiers.* A blonde in a convertible? Before she could move, I gave her another one. And pulled a face. And cocked a snoot. I breathed fire. If they were looking for trouble, they'd come to the right man. An old lady in a Fiat? Too bad, Granny. *Et vlan!* I was having a whale of a time. Give the French what they deserve.

Exhausted, but morally vindicated, I arrived in the car park in front of *Lots-Lots*. A hoarding announced a fresh arrival of bed linen. Tremendous. This time last year I had bought a duvet cover with an attractive palm-tree motif but the coconuts had since faded. Time for a change. By now I was in a good mood. Bullish, I left the car, turned round to close the doors. And stopped. Horrified.

Overcome, petrified with shame.

What did I see on the roof of the car?

My shoes.

I'd come back with my shopping, perched the shoes on the car to look for the keys, and driven off. Everyone I'd met in Loches that afternoon had been making a kindly, concerned gesture with their finger, lifting it courteously in my direction. 'You've left your shoes on the roof!'

I was appalled. What a start to my year.

After Fashoda and Mers el Khébir, Loches.

2

Love is a tricky business. Phèdre, in the excellent verse drama penned several centuries ago by my confrère Jean Racine, put the whole thing in an Alexandrine and a nutshell:

C'est Vénus tout entière à sa proie attachée.

I wouldn't go quite so far as to say that the Goddess of Love was out to nobble me personally, but life was fraught with new complications. The *coup de foudre* – the thunderbolt which is the French metaphor for love at first sight – does *sui generis* take you by surprise. Hiding in a bathroom at a fancy-dress party in the pretty village of Pont de Ruan dressed as Margaret Thatcher I was hardly expecting to come across the love of my life. But I did. And there was no going back.

Of course, on occasions, one rubs one's eyes and asks oneself, Did it really happen? Lou Charpin, I had in fact only met once since the thunderbolt. During the grape harvest we had dinner under the shade of age-old chestnut trees at the Grand Vatel in Vouvray. I ate an *andouillette* – a complex and transgressional sausage having some none too distant an acquaintance with a pig's innards – and *girolles*, wild mushrooms tasting of autumn. The meal was accompanied by Vouvray in its various guises – *sec, tendre* – a more blowsy version of dry – *demi-sec*, the half-brother of the former and *moelleux*, the lush mellow rich cousin. Ever since – and

absence has increased the frequency of day dreaming –
I had associated my beautiful Tourangelle with these
tastes, which Lou found highly complimentary as con-
cerns the wine but less so in respect of the sausage.
It was on that occasion that I made my declaration.
I was going to return to England, pack up, chuck it all
in, return to France and live eternally at her feet (bottle
three).

'*Quelle fougue*, Mike,' she replied.

And *fougue* I went for. At the time I didn't quite
follow but the dictionary confirmed my contentment:
ardour, spirit; *fougueux*: mettlesome, fiery, hot-headed.
Lou made me mettlesome. *Fougue*. I might even make
an art of it.

'*Vous, les Anglais, vraiment . . .*'

She was right. After the Latin lover . . . the *rosbif*
Romeo!

I returned to Abesbury late September. The thatched
semi in the village was rented. No problem on that
score. I made a gift of my petunias to the next-door
neighbour Mrs Trevor, whose poodle was peeing the
privet hedge to death (no longer my concern), my
Industrial Revolution mower to the vicar, the only man
in the village polite enough not to say no, and my plum
jam to a jumble sale to Save the Kangaroo.

This was not the first time I had left for ever. My
university colleagues were getting tired of my farewell
performances. I was like a dipsy diva. Worse. The
whole of England seemed to be packing its bags and
leaving for France, the candidates lining up on the cliffs
of Dover like swallows on September telegraph wires.
The milkman, passionate about wine, had left to brew
his own poison in Béziers, the man from the bookshop
to rear mussels in Brittany and the grocer to organize a

traffic in Weetabix and Marmite in the Périgord noir. Soon there would be no one left. After the ghost town, the ghost island.

My Swindon friends eyed me with a mixture of admiration and compassion. What about job security? And National Insurance? And the pension? To hell with it. To them the Minutes, the arse-licking and the warm beer. To me the rosé and the *religieuses* (no, not nuns, buns). To each his adventure.

A small do was organized to celebrate my new departure. It was held in the refectory whose stark, concrete walls were impregnated by the stench of years of mashed potato. I was given a small cheque, a pat on the back and a glass of flat champagne. I replied with a speech that sought to bubble.

What kind of witchcraft, I asked rhetorically, had been performed on this courteous, crumpled but well-matured Oxonian to explain his curious desire to abandon his country, culture, cricket and tea for a land inhabited by natives incapable of pronouncing 'th' without wetting the wallpaper, who drink port before the meal and who overtake on the right and on the left both on the highway and in politics. Answer? *L'amour.*

The Faculty clearly thought I was losing my marbles. Love is a fragile commodity, evanescent, treacherous. Re-read your classics, dear Michael. *All that glitters is not gold.* Keen to convince, throwing caution and truth to the winds, I had recourse to elementary lyricism. If Keats got away with it, why not me?

I was leaving to marry, I boasted. In fact, I was about to say 'wed' but thought it a shade too nineteenth century, changed the word into 'marry' at the last moment, and it came out 'warry'. They got the gist.

I didn't want to be too fulsome but in fact I was getting married the . . . Here I mumbled a grunt faintly resembling a date followed by another grunt faintly resembling a month. The announcement led the hitherto dubious assembly to melt into sentimentality like sugar in a glass of absinthe (which, as we all know, makes the heart grow fonder). 'Why didn't you tell us before, Michael? Wonderful news! *Félicitations*,' etc. The reaction was so heartfelt that I lost control. Fantasy slipped behind the wheel and I elaborated – choosing the best man and the rings, designing the wedding dress, kissing the bridesmaids, selecting the music – a smoochy 'L'Été Indien' by Joe Dassin – and last but not least renting Maigret's black Citroën to drive us to the reception. *Quelle fête!*

Both the assembly and myself were very moved. So romantic! All that remained was to hire the Cinderella coach, ring the Seven Dwarves and . . . ask Lou Charpin.

I stuffed a few files in a bag, hugged the copious librarian, whose bosom had provided an attractive alternative to study, spat on the wheels of the Porsche belonging to Badger, the Head of Department who found France old hat, and *au revoir la compagnie!*

I was to cross the frontier of my new life at Newhaven, the port of no return. To mark the solemnity of the moment I did two laps of the inner ring road, waving farewell to the pleasant Chinese couple who ran the chip shop, blowing a kiss in the direction of the flea-market, and breathing in the nostalgic pong from the distant fresh fish shop.

The pride of the Transmanche Ferries line awaited in harbour, a vast yellow hulk looking like a floating money box. Avoiding the liquid gathering in the

Flaubert Bar, where my compatriots were helping each other hoist their bellies on to the Formica counter, I made my way up, via a freshly painted rusty staircase, to the open-air disco on the promenade deck painted in its psychedelic cream and orange stripes. Perched on a mushroom-shaped bar stool bolted to the deck – perfect for sipping Bacardi in storms – as the yellow scrapheap heaved its way laboriously out of the harbour accompanied by a chorus of wailing seagulls, I contemplated my past slipping away before my eyes.

When I was small, my parents would take me in my pram to the beach at Newhaven. The ascent of the pebble dunes was tough but when we reached the top, pleasure rewarded the effort. My father would stop, puffed, take a deep breath and facing the sea, inhale.

A slight breeze seemed at first to carry nothing but the stench of diesel fuel and old seaweed. But a gust from the south, blowing in from the invisible coast of Dieppe straight opposite us, began to tickle our noses with something a shade more magic.

'Pastis,' said my father. 'I can smell pastis.'

Better still, a smell deeper, blacker, rich and bitter, began to displace the aniseed apéritif.

Un petit noir ... Coffee. Intense shots of jet-black coffee, served on zinc counters in small cups to a cigarette-smoking kebab of workmen in *bleu de travail* lined up against the bar. Newhaven disappeared. Standing on the very hem of England, facing south across the Channel, their backs turned away from the water-pastures of the Ouse Valley, my parents drank an invisible coffee and smoked an invisible Gauloise. They inhaled France.

The French dream lives on. I am in the *potager*, the

vegetable garden, of my country house in the Touraine.
The bees hum Charles Trenet in the vine. Lou Charpin,
Madame Sadler, her mass of black hair tumbling down
her slender naked back, is making backcurrant jam in a
copper pan in the kitchen while our fifteen children play
happily in the garden. I sip a glass of fresh rosé from the
estate and put the final touches to my new novel, which
the press is eager to salute as a masterpiece, when, with
diabolical precision, a seagull craps down the neck of
my shirt.

My arrival in France is traditionally celebrated by the
purchase of a Livarot, the vast fat paunchy pouf of a
cheese, looking like an oversize Camembert, with its
love handles and its orange crumbly crust. My personal
supplier in Dieppe plies his trade in the rue Victor
Hugo, where his creamy flock slowly mature in the
shadow of the Eglise St Jacques.
    Together we selected the victim. Ripe, welcoming
but not overweeningly enthusiastic. Box in hand – a
smiling cow in conversation with an affable monk
holding a milking stool – I made my way to the beach.
When opening a Livarot, take care not to find yourself
in an enclosed space. Car parks, moors or deserts are
recommended. Once you have ensured that downwind
of the box there are no young children or elderly people
in fragile health, open it, unwrap the cheese from its
embossed paper and admire its plump girth in its corset
of *laîches**. Undo the bondage using a penknife
specially reserved for the purpose (the stink, remember,

* *Une laîche* is a hernia-belt to support blowsy fat cheeses – one of
my favourite useless words. It is because of the five bands of *laîches*
that a *Livarot* is commonly called *un colonel*.

is indelible) and then, in a moment of great sensuality, sink your teeth into the colonel's bum.

My parents would inhale France. I devoured it.

3

Lou Charpin, the future Madame Sadler, was on the phone. Her voice? An enchanting mixture of Jeanne Moreau, Catherine Deneuve and Sophie Marceau all rolled into bed. My knees melted.

It was arranged that I would go to pick her up at her parents' house in St Radégonde, a residential suburb of Tours, on Sunday after lunch. Like a candidate for one of the forty seats amongst the 'immortals' of the *Académie Française* I was to begin to do the rounds. In the weeks and months to come, Lou would introduce me to her family, her friends, her dog, if she had one. I would be surveyed, assessed, judged. Dry rot, subsidence, liability to flood would be observed, boxes would be ticked, reports would be signed. No stone would be left unturned. I seized the gauntlet. The *rosbif* must be found acceptable in the searching eyes of the *Académie Charpin*.

A real professional, I prepared painstakingly for the audition. After a lot of ooh-ing and aah-ing – I had at least two jackets from which to choose – I opted to wear a crumpled linen number for its destructured, intellectual look and, inspired by an ad in an old copy of *Elle* I'd found in the barn depicting a gentleman farmer loading a Labrador into a Land Rover – a pair of worn cord trousers for what I would call '*le look grunge*'.

The costume was one hurdle. The script was the

next. Preparation was essential. What did Lou Charpin do as a day job when she wasn't eating *andouillettes* with me? Top executive? Top model? No. Lou Charpin was an *agrégée de grammaire*. The *agrégation* is France's most demanding and competitive exam. If you win, you are the best. Lou was a top grammarian. Every time I opened my mouth I was in danger. I went to bed at night repeating the rules. *Avant que* followed by the subjunctive. *Après que* by the indicative. When I got it wrong I was punished. But when I got it right, I was knocking on heaven's door.

Il eût fallu que tu me caressasses (it would have been necessary for you to caress me) won an extremely pleasant afternoon of the aforesaid activity.

The rendezvous was for half past three. I arrived at half past two to give myself time to explore the terrain and to practise my opening gambits *in situ*. St Radégonde has real provincial charm: the kind of oddly assembled Lego-style villas you associate with nineteenth-century seaside resorts, tucked up behind overrun gardens, complete with unkempt willows, hirsute hedging and badly groomed umbrella pines.

Allée Notre Dame was a shady cul-de-sac. Ten houses on the right, eight on the left plus a convent – La Chapelle des Sœurs Notre-dame. This particular Sunday afternoon there were cars parked every-where – a dirty BMW, a Renault Espace stuffed full of Barbies, a sparkling Twingo, a beaten-up Golf with an *I ♥ Bulgaria* sticker, and a Trabant with a teddy bear, wearing an unusual red sweater sporting the hammer and sickle, hanging from the driving mirror. My first contact with my future family-in-law.

In order to park I was obliged to drive the Mazda into the privet hedge – the only space left – scratching my nostril as I squeezed out of the car. A loud, angry voice sounded behind me as a red-faced apoplectic neighbour stormed out of number 22. He stopped and surveyed the herd of vehicles belonging to the Charpin family and swore very politely.

'*Non de nom!*' Either it was the seventeenth of the month or it wasn't.

He explained his anguish. Every week of the month, you park on a different side of the road. From the first to the seventh: on the left. From the eighth to the sixteenth, on the right. *Simple, non? Semaines paires* (even numbers), right; *semaines impaires* (odd numbers), left. I didn't dare let on that, until recently, confusing *impaire* with *imper* (meaning raincoat but pronounced the same) I thought *une semaine impaire* was a week when the weather was bad.

Mrs Apoplectic, a large blonde Madame wearing a pink fluffy housecoat, appeared on the street to lend support, joined by a thin green bean of a neighbour with a beret and shears whose head I had espied peering over a beech hedge. Together, looking in disgust at the anarchic parking, we lamented the decline of Western Civilization. *Ah, mon cher monsieur, je ne vous dis pas . . .*

Then, suddenly, a miracle. A bell tolled in the convent and, like a divine emissary, a nun in a blue pinny popped out. We all performed a variant upon the genuflection, the nun embraced us in her angelic smile and the road rage immediately abated. I understood. The Chapel was the headquarters of a special order of parking nuns.

Before me, the address I had so often dreamed about: number 14, Allée Notre Dame, the family home, the

centrepoint, the fountainhead, *casa nostra*. Beyond
the thick crumbling stone walls lay a large, attractively
rundown family house with faded pink brick around
the windows, pastel-green shutters, guttering which
looked as if it had been installed by a loony ecologist,
and Virginia creeper used as a ladder for cats, bedding
for birds and as a kind of green hairnet for a house
which, without it, was in danger, not necessarily of
falling down, but of losing one or two of its extremities.

Before ringing the bell in the wall, I recrumpled the
linen grunge look and practised my first line:

'*Monsieur et Madame Charpin, quelle joie im-
mense . . .*' Then I stopped. It all sounded unnatural,
constipated, over-rehearsed. *Merde.*

'*C'est avec une sincère excitation et respect que . . .*'
Even worse. But I could hardly say, '*Salut les copains!*'
(Hey, dudes?) Even to my untrained ears, this sounded
a shade over the top.

I eventually rang the bell, trusting that adrenalin
would induce something more acceptable to pop out
in spite of myself. No one heard. From the other side
of the wall, the sound of a French family lunch in
full swing. I paused in anticipation of enchantment,
expecting scraps of song, conversations about Sartre,
an Alexandrine or two. What I actually heard sounded
more like a free-for-all.

'*Mais non!*'

'*Quelle idée!*'

'*C'est pas possible!*'

They were doubtless deep in the thralls of a political
discussion. This is what the French do at lunch. We
Brits nervously stick a Lib Dem poster in the bathroom
window in a place where no one can see it. Not the
French. No, sir. They tear each other apart. They throw

their hands up in the air. They slam their fists down on the table. From the other side of the wall I could feel the temperature rising. Maybe this was not after all the best time to be introduced. I was about to back off and once again to stick the privet twigs up my nose when the door in the wall opened and Lou appeared. She was wearing a waisted short jacket and tight satin trousers, tucked into boots. Her beauty halted my retreat.

'Why are you walking backwards?' she asked.

'I was just—'

'*Entrez. Viens.* We were just having a row.'

What I presumed was the whole family were assembled outdoors under the *tonnelle* – the bower. Lunch was over. Bottles of eau de vie de prune et Armagnac rubbed shoulders with teapots of limeflower tisane. The crust of a plum tart was fed to a dog, someone had just dropped an apricot on his trousers, jackets were tossed over the backs of the slatted wooden garden furniture, thick curls of tobacco smoke furled upwards into the roses, children were dismantling a plastic doll. My heart beat fast. I was at last on stage.

I uttered my first line: '*Bonjour mesdames, messieurs.*'

Lou, sensing that the script wasn't up to scratch, introduced me herself. '*Je vous présente Michael.*'

The assembly turned to examine me, politely, compassionately, a shade sardonically. I had the impression that they had seen all this before. Lou's suitors probably passed every Sunday with the *pousse-café*. Remember the Lithuanian with a lisp? And the giant Swede who hit his head on the gazebo? They paused in mid-flight and greeted me with an affable, amused: '*Bonjour, monsieur.*'

Monsieur? Who did they take me for? A British

brush salesman? And then they resumed where they had
left off before being rudely interrupted.

'*Ça ne va pas, non!*'

'*Quelle idée saugrenue!!!*'

Lou sighed, took my arm and faced the assembly.
'Let's just agree to disagree, OK? *Salut la compagnie.
On va au ciné.*'

And we were outside! I felt *lésé*: short-shrifted. All
that rehearsal, all that scriptwriting, all that grunge
dressing for a smile and a *bonjour*. The rift must have
been a deep one.

'What was that all about?' I asked rather sulkily.

'All that what?'

'All that argument.'

'Oh, that was nothing. We were arguing. *Et
alors?* That's what families do. In this instance we were
arguing about the *clafoutis*.'

French politics, I was aware, is a minefield of
acronyms. They have to be mastered or nothing is
comprehensible: UMP, PCF, PS, PC. CLAFOUTIS
must be yet another one. But what? *Cellule Léniniste
Anti-Fasciste de Tendance International-Socialiste?*

Lou sensed I was lagging behind. '*Le Clafoutis*', she
explained. 'The flan.'

Flan? *Merde.* '*Fédération Lilloise Anti-Nucléaire?*'

Lou ruffled my hair. 'The flan. The dessert. The
cherry tart.'

Why get so hot under the collar about a tart?

'My younger sister Cécile left the stones in the
cherries.'

'So?'

Lou sighed. Would the English never come to grips
with life's essentials?

'*Tu es charmant, Mike,*' she said gently, 'but you

have a lot to learn. I'll explain. One half of the family leaves the stones in the cherries because stones lend a nutty taste to the tart. The other half removes them because they are too chic to spit *C'est clair?*'

The film was *Pierrot-le-fou* by Jean-Luc Godard. A new, remastered copy. Lou identified with the character of Marianne played by Anna Karina, who spends the whole film proving particularly elusive. I had the distinct impression that the reels were shown in the wrong order, but very much appreciated the end when Ferdinand paints his face blue and explodes himself with red dynamite. If Lou proved too elusive, I'd do the same.

In the warm summer twilight we strolled along the Boulevard Bérenger. Tours is divided by a long, tree-lined boulevard only interrupted by the central Place du Palais: the more severe Boulevard Heurteloup to the east and the more romantic Boulevard Bérenger to the west. Lou took my arm, stopped, and for the first time we kissed chastely in public, the squirrel of the savings bank the *Caisse d'Epargne* standing in for Cupid.

I would have been happy to spend the whole evening parading nonchalantly up and down the boulevard, stopping only to make the squirrel blush, but Lou had some important matter to settle. I left her at the Salamandre, a smart old-style bar all baroque wood panelling and flowery wallpaper. I wanted to speak to her about my novel, her jam and our fifteen children, but I knew I must learn to be patient.

I walked back to the trusty Mazda waiting for me under the plane trees of the Boulevard Heurteloup and was in the process of courteously backing out of the

parking place when a vast black four-wheel drive
flashed its headlights at me. What was wrong? Apparently, I was too slow. The driver threw his hands in
the air, exasperated.

'*Mais qu'est-ce qu'ils foutent, ces Anglais!*' he
gestured, before taking another place a whole twenty
yards further up the boulevard.

As the driver slammed his door, my body stiffened.
Our eyes met, but he didn't recognize me. This wasn't
surprising. The only time he had ever seen me before,
I was dressed as Margaret Thatcher. But I knew who
he was. He was none other than Gérard Mortier the
optician, Lou's ex. The man whose Vouvray '47 we had
emptied in the bathroom at the fancy-dress party at Pont
de Ruan. Once the Latin lover, now the Latin loser.

Or so I had thought. What was *he* doing in Tours on
a Sunday evening? Why was *he* in such a hurry?
Assailed by a terrible gnawing anxiety, I followed
him. Along the pedestrian rue de Bordeaux he didn't
even stop to admire the attractive display of Terylene
trousers in the window of Brummell Hommes. A sixth
sense told me where he was going, and I wasn't wrong.
He turned the corner of the Place du Palais and without
hesitation disappeared into the panelled warmth of
the Salamandre bar.

Le ciel me tombe sur la tête. The sky fell on my nut.
I was gobsmacked.

An important matter to see to, *mon œil!* Clearly
Gérard had not stepped out of Lou's life and his star
was less in the wane than I had thought. My vain-
glorious speech in Swindon rang ironically in my ears.
The ring, the wedding list, the bridesmaids. I had spoken
too soon. The gods, miffed by my hubris, had decided
to slap me on the wrist.

What could I do? Paint my face blue and light the touch paper?

Non, monsieur. An Englishman's honour was at stake.

The Grand Slam International Tournament had only just begun.

4

Since my return from England to my village in the Touraine, I hadn't seen much of the Toison mafia.

In the Super-U, our neighbourhood supermarket, I bumped into Penthouse who was filling his caddie with provisions – tuna-fish rillettes (30% extra for free), five-yard-long Breton all-butter cakes with prunes, and boxes of a deep-frozen chocolate and vanilla concoction, of which the village was apparently very fond, which looked like a power station in the snow and was called a Viennetta. The Tasmalou were having a bash in the presbytery on the fifteenth of the month.

The world is composed of tribes: the tribes of Judah, the Mongols, the Slavs, the Saxons. Centuries ago, many of these nomads decided to stop being on the road. They took off their clogs, put their knapsacks in the wardrobe, found a bed for the horse, married the daughter of the local grocer and called it a day. That's how nations were born. The ancient tribe of Toison, the Tasmalou, consists of Penthouse – so named for his taste in light reading; Nestor the baker with his fermenting yeast in a blue plastic bucket; La Varice the plumber, with his eye-catching varicose veins; Pois-Chiche the handyman, famous for planting the flag of Venezuela in the municipal flowerbed; and Henri, the once acrobatic roof carpenter, whose balancing acts are now limited to dramatic feats between cup and lip.

A colourful bunch, their hides are tanned by years of
bad weather and seasons spent toiling behind a plough
horse that farts. Average age: seventy-three.

The present condition of the Tasmalou was evident
as soon as you arrived at the presbytery. In ancient
times you would have had to wend your way through
the horses tied to the iron rings still set in the wall.
More recently, the courtyard had been a jumble of prehistoric bicycles with their fat orange tyres. Nowadays
the entrance was a maze of Zimmer frames, looking
like a lot of metallic spiders having a gangbang.

The presbytery itself had recently been refurbished,
thanks to a grant from the Conseil Régional. What
had once been a large ancient room with gnarled beams
and a huge fireplace had been turned into a centrally
heated, plastic echo-chamber. The flagstones had been
replaced by grey, synthetic, booze-resistant tiles. You
spilled a bottle of Bourgeuil and hop! A quick squirt
of Mir (a French cleaning agent, not a space station)
and in a flash it was as spick as span. The whole place,
in the words of Penthouse, had become 100 per cent
'Fornica'. You whispered a secret in the ear of your
neighbour and you could be heard on the church square
in Mouzay, five kilometres away. The acoustic made
the town-crier redundant.

On the day of the party, no one took any notice of
me when I entered. The room was packed, the festivities
in full swing. A parlour game was being played. In
the middle of the Mir-cleaned floor was an empty
chair. Sitting next to it was Nestor, acting as referee.
The game began. Pois-Chiche stood up and crossed the
floor, walking slowly under the close scrutiny of his
colleagues. He then sat on the empty chair, crossed
his right leg over his left, then the left over the right. He

stood up again and walked sedately back to his place. Nestor started to take bets.

'*OK. Il les a? Ou il ne les a pas?*' He's got them? He hasn't got them?

The company had thirty seconds to choose. Three in favour, thirty against. Pois-Chiche smiled broadly. He'd taken them in.

'*Je les ai!*' he chortled. I've got them!

'Got what?' I enquired of my nearest neighbour, who looked at me as if I'd landed from the moon.

'*Les hémorroïdes, pardi!*'

Pois-Chiche had piles. This was the game which had given its name to the tribe:

'*T'as mal où?*'

'*J'ai mal au cul.*'

And everyone fell about laughing. In this way, ill-health and decrepitude have redesigned the Toison party scene. In February it will be the cholesterol rave. In April the gout knees-up.

As they passed around thick chunks of Viennetta, washed down with a cloying Chardonnay, they waxed nostalgic, talking of *l'amour* – the blacksmith from Dolus who had kept his wife locked in the wardrobe, the baker from Varennes who had cooked his in the bread oven and, one thing leading to another, they began to tickle me about my own lovelife.

'*Alors, Michel?*'

'*Hein?*'

'*On est tout seul?*'

'*Hein?*'

'*Et la petite copine?*'

I'd told them too much. It was the Swindon Syndrome. Desperate to convince myself, I'd opened my big mouth. But I certainly wasn't going to let on about the unctuous optician seen disappearing into the Salamander bar.

'*Ça avance, ça avance,*' I said airily.

The tribe was in dire need of fresh blood. In the last few years there had been only two newcomers in the village: a stonemason and his girlfriend. They lived together but had grown-up children by other marriages. She worked at the old people's home, where he was building the new wing. The Tasmalou had only one hope. Marcellin.

Squat, plump and bashful, Marcellin, the owner and sole employee of the N'Garage in Mouzay, was a meticulous bachelor; the front seats of his immaculate Citroën Picasso were always protected by plastic covers. For reasons which I had never fathomed, a large flamboyant red N was painted above the main entrance to his premises, lending the establishment a somewhat exotic Afro-Tibetan touch: the N'Garage. But Marcellin's deep secret was his unrequited passion.

In term-time, early every morning and late every afternoon, Marcellin's car, like a doting pilot fish, wended its way from village to village, from farm to cottage, following the trail of the school bus. Was Marcellin anticipating a breakdown? No, sir. Marcellin was in love. Monique Bourdeau, who had arrived in the area some two years ago, was married to Louis, a dapper mechanic who worked on a North Sea oil rig. To while away the long days and nights, his wife, who had her heavy vehicle *permis B*, applied to drive the school bus. Ever since, Monique, a voluptuous blonde in her forties, as lush and edible as an overripe pear, would bus local children from home to primary school and back again. And Marcellin would follow behind her, ignoring the brats in the back window who, like impudent fish in an aquarium, would flutter their hands over their heart, play imaginary violins and blow passionate kisses in the direction of the devoted, taciturn lover in his plastic-seated Picasso.

Taciturn was his problem. Marcellin couldn't bring himself to declare his passion. Like a hothouse orchid in a secret garden, his love remained bottled up. The Tasmalou chafed at the bit. Henri raised his pockmarked red and blue nose to the sky, breathed in the air of the village and summed up the situation with precision and poetry.

'*Ça manque de copulation dans le canton.*'

Leaving the presbytery I did a tour of Toison to walk off the large helpings of Viennetta. On the façades of the houses were faded painted signs of past glories: the Café de la Poste, the Café de la Paix, le Café de Georgette, Anselme the *bourrelier* – the mattress-maker – two grocers and the blacksmith. All that remained was the bakery. Shops had been converted into houses and the houses, in turn, had been abandoned. In Provence there is a tradition of *transhumance*. In summer, livestock travel to the high mountain pastures to escape the heat of the plain. In Toison *la transhumance* works differently. In winter the elderly villagers leave for the hospice in Ligueil. Soon they'll all be siphoned off, the inhabitants on one side of the hill and their houses on the other.

Later on that afternoon, when the party was over, I went for a walk with the Tasmalou on the hills overlooking Toison. Le Père Maurice died three years ago. His vine was abandoned, wild grass growing along the wire trellis and suffocating the gnarled *ceps*. His wine used to be wonderful. 'Le Poison de Toison' they called it.

In silence we looked down at the village, smoke curling up from too few chimneys.

'*Alors, Michel?*'

'*Ce mariage?*'

'*Ça avance. Ça avance.*'

5

The telephone rang. A rare occurrence. I was knee-deep in conversation with the leeks at the bottom of the garden and had to run into the house with thick mud clinging to my boots, trying to hide the heavy breathing which, had the caller been Lou, might have been taken for excessive excitement.

It wasn't. It was Gisèle, Lou's sister-in-law, married to Laurent, the brother who ran a computer firm in the *zone industrielle* of Loches and who spent his time looking after the well-being of the local branch of the Franco-Bulgarian League of Friendship.

My morale was boosted by having a member of the Charpin family on the phone. Someone had had the kindness to notice me when I made my rapid first appearance under the family arbour. As Gisèle introduced herself I had time to consult the family tree I had stuck on the wall. Gisèle worked for the BNP bank and was responsible for the *coins de confidentialité*: Confidentiality Corners – little counters tucked away behind rubber plants where you own up to having bought a stuffed camel on credit – the banking equivalent of the confessional. In the present instance it was Gisèle who sought to unload herself. We arranged a rendezvous at a newly opened tea room in Loches called *Le Kosey Korner*.

Wearing a black jacket and trousers and with her

hair, tinted the colour of burned marmalade, pulled back in a tight chignon, Gisèle was very much the businesswoman. She was accompanied by Ernesto, a large, dribbling Alsatian, who immediately started flatulating under the table. A waitress in a pinny brought us the menu which featured an extraordinary choice of exotic teas: bergamot tea, coconut tea, plum tea. I personally would have preferred chinon tea but it wasn't on offer.

After the usual courteous opening gambits – the weather, the Queen, Alsatians and their digestive system – we got down to the nitty gritty. Gisèle lowered her voice. Her problem – no, her obsession – was her son, Dylan. He was eighteen and in danger of failing his *Baccalauréat*. Gisèle opened her briefcase and took out a folder of school reports. His gym teacher had spotted the danger – *le hic* – as early as the second form: Dylan was, apparently, a gifted child if he would care to take the trouble. There was the rub. He wouldn't get up in the morning. Gisèle had tried the lot – Crunchies, Weetabix, muesli, Country Store and a gamut of other breakfast cereals – raspberry-flavoured, blackcurrant-flavoured, bacon-flavoured, *coq au vin*-flavoured – you name it. In vain. Dylan would remain open-mouthed and inert in his bed. The bait didn't work. The fish couldn't give a fart.

Why? asked Gisèle rhetorically. Why should he refuse to get up? Why, at his tender age, should he refuse to sink his teeth into the apple of life?

Gisèle looked around at the other ladies in the room politely sipping their infusions. The *verveine*? *Her* daughter had got a Distinction in Science. The green tea and a slice of apple tart? *Her* son had a Merit in Literature. The family reputation was at stake.

What would people think if Dylan failed? Would Gisèle still be consultable behind her rubber plants? *Ah, le standing* . . .

She finally arrived at the crux of the matter. Would I, an English scholar and a gentleman, be able to find an odd moment to give Dylan a little private instruction? *King Lear* was on the programme. None of them could understand it. She'd read it. Laurent had read it. Ernesto had read it. In vain. The text remained beyond their ken.

Sipping my walnut tea, I was sensitive to her dismay. Particularly so because pleasing Gisèle could be a means of pleasing Lou.

'*Il est si gentil, ce Mikaël. Et si intelligent. Et si disponible* . . .'

It was also a good way of poking the unctuous Gérard Mortier in the eye. No one is going to turn to a provincial optician to resolve the literary problems of their Oblomov of a son. I accepted gracefully. Of course I'd give a hand. Gisèle and Ernesto were deeply thankful.

At the door, Gisèle took my arm. 'You'll see, Michael. He is so charming. He loves Flemish art and canaries.'

Ah bon?

In order to prepare for the classes I read *King Lear* myself. I saw what they meant. *Ce n'est pas de la tarte*, as the French nicely put it. It's not easy. The plot tells the story of an aging loony king seeking to share out his kingdom between his three daughters. The dialogue is written in blank, wild, dense, complex verse. How could I communicate this to a wanker who wasn't even excited by the prospect of Weetabix?

Dylan was my first French teenager. *Mon premier*

ado. 'A new world', as Dvorak might have put it in Czech. I decided to do some research. At Le Palais, a big café in the centre of Tours, I pursued my studies. There were two species. The boys wore jeans with a low-slung crutch, the girls tighter versions of the same, stopping on their hips, just short of becoming extremely interesting. The girls had rucksacks. Not the boys, who clearly stored their school equipment in the under-carriage compartment. I transcribed scraps of dialogue for later analysis.

'Je kiffe pas le keum.'
'C'est grand.'
*'C'est chez qui, la teuf?'**
Worse than *King Lear*.

I bought a copy of *Too much: le magazine trop bien* and took notes on the heartaches of Lady Laistee the Queen of Rap, the tour dates of Diam's, the managerial switch of Stan etc. Electrifying. I then lis-tened to the new CD of the infamous NTM (whose extremely Freudian acronym *Nique Ta Mère* means 'screw your mother'), learning at the same time to pars the verb *niquer*: *je nique, tu niques, il nique*. And the subjunctive: *il faudrait que nous niquassions* (it would be necessary for us to screw, etc).

Once prepared, I made my way to the *pavillon* – detached house – standing behind its white-painted concrete fence in a suburb of Loches. The garden was all pebbles and bushes with red imitation plastic berries. I rang the bell. Ernesto the farting Alsatian announced my arrival by throwing himself against the front door like a starved wolf.

---

* It turned out to be *verlan* – the hip slang formed by saying words wardsback: *keum = mec* = bloke; *teuf = fête* = party. And so on.

'*Il est con, ce klebs,*' said a voice. *Klebs* must be a dog.

Dylan opened the door, dressed for the Vietnam War in a flak-jacket, camouflage trousers and a Johnny Depp goatee. While Ernesto continued to slaver over the walls, Dylan ushered me into the kitchen, which was decorated with posters advertising Beautiful Bulgaria.

'*Fait chier,*' Dylan grunted, and threw the dog out into the garden. He was in the middle of making himself a sandwich.

'*Tu veux du Nutella?*'

I declined, but the *tutoiement* was a welcome, friendly touch. Dylan took his sandwich, went straight to his room, took a book off the shelf and sat behind his desk.

'*Merci.*'

Why he said thank you I had no idea but clearly he was used to having private lessons. I looked around surreptitiously. The bedroom was littered with the remnants of discarded whims and hobbies – a piano and a few unlikely-looking scores – one named *Les Violettes* – a guitar with three strings, a riding helmet with a Mylène Farmer transfer and a recorder obviously virgin of any labial contact.

Two props stood out. On the wall, a poster of a Vermeer painting. On the table, a birdcage containing three overweight canaries. Not overweight. Obese. This predilection for Flemish art and for Sumo canaries was intriguing. Did he force-feed his birds? Was canary *foie-gras* the nec plus ultra of *le fooding*? – as the French call hip eating.

'*Alors, King Lear?*' I began. 'What do you think of the hero? *Comment tu le trouves?*'

Dylan adjusted his undercarriage and said nothing. Then: *'C'est un vieux con. Un pédophile.'*

How the world has changed. A century ago, a young student expressing himself in this way would have been cut into small pieces and roasted on the fire for lunch. Nowadays, any reaction is a blessing. I shelved my knife.

'And his daughters?' I went on.

'Des pétasses.' Fortunately I had done my homework. *Pétasses.* Stupid, mindless girls.

'Pourquoi "pétasses"?'

'Elles parlent trop.'

I hastened to point out that, had the daughters not spoken, there would have been no play. Dylan seemed to like the idea.

'Tant mieux,' he mumbled.

'Pourquoi?'

'Il fait chier.'

Dylan clearly lumped Shakespeare and Ernesto in the same basket. Somewhat put out by the harshness of his reading, I ventured to ask if there was nothing in the play he liked.

'Si.'

Ah. And what precisely would that be?

'Lorsqu'on éborgne le mec.'

I had suspected it. The eye-gouging scene.

'C'est gore.'

I was lost. Dylan looked at me in disdain. I didn't go for the gory? Who was this old fart who was trying to pick up his aunt? We didn't even speak the same language. I told him the story of the play but he took no notes, proceeding merely to eat his Nutella sandwich and to clean his nose. As I left, in an attempt to be sympathetic I put my finger in the fat canary cage but the birds were either too blasé or too bloated to respond.

0 out of 10.

If Dylan votes in the Académie Charpin, I'm sunk.

6

A moment of great excitement. I was to take my first hesitant steps in Touraine society. Lou had invited me to a dinner with her colleagues from the Lycée Albert Camus.

Just to be exhibited in public was in itself gratifying. To be the perfect guest I decided to buy a small gift. I was about to purchase a bunch of sweet peas – Lou's favourite flowers – when I hesitated. She might find me too sycophantic. So I bought the vase instead. This was my first vase. Narrow at the base, widening and becoming bluer as it went upwards.

'Il est curieux, ton vase.'

Lou was dressed gypsy style in a deep-red pleated silk skirt, with a green bandana in her jet-black hair, her eyes flashing as if she was Carmen. *Curieux* must be her way of saying *moche*, or crap.

Cedric and Marylène Pinson lived in a *pavillon* near the Beffroi, a *quartier* to the north of Tours. When they had first bought their house, they were surrounded by fields, but the town had rapidly encroached on their pastoral bliss. Smart blocks of flats – *des immeubles de standing* – grew like mushrooms in fields where mushrooms once grew. The garden suffered from lack of sun. With four storeys on the left, they moved the vegetable garden to the right. Six storeys to the right, they moved it to the front. Four storeys at the front, they shifted it to the back. Soon they were going to have to plant their asparagus on the roof.

The garden was at present encumbered by piles of freshly cut three-year-old wood covered in blue plastic sheeting. Rosebushes on tiptoe desperately sought a breath of fresh air. The door was opened by Cedric Pinson, a Maths teacher and an *agrégé*. He was tall and thin, wearing ankle socks, flip-flops – *des tongs* – smoking a pipe and surrounded by an army of babies wearing Pampers disposable nappies. They slid over the floor behind him on their plastic bums. Lou and I stepped carefully over the babies and made our way to the salon where I was to be introduced.

Marylène, the mother of the Pampers division, Cedric's wife and a History *agrégée*, gave me an extremely warm kiss on both cheeks. She was wearing a post-Woodstock smock dress, had an Afro hairdo, bulging eyes and made her own bread. Slumped horizontally next to her in a leather scoop chair was Bertrand the Philosophy *agrégé*, complete with high forehead and regulation gold-rimmed specs.

'No successful dinner-party in France can be held without a Trotskyite,' said Lou. They had apparently hired Bertrand from InterTrot.

Béatrice, an education counsellor, an attractive auburn-haired woman in a Zara-style imitation Chanel, spent her time removing the bottle of wine from the clutches of her soak of a bearded husband Denis, the German *agrégé*. Serge, the Gym *agrégé*, all muscle and bounce, was accompanied by Gretchen, the German *Lektorin*, with her plaits and leather miniskirt. Denis kept dropping Chipsters on the floor so that she would have to bend down and pick them up, thereby revealing an attractive vista of her Bavarian origins. Serge was lecturing us on the CIRPP which, after the *clafoutis*, I took to be a dessert, but which turned out to be an Inter-Regional Ping Pong Competition (*Le Concours Inter-Régional de Ping-Pong*).

The staffroom was keen to have a shufty at the new man in the life of Lou Charpin and so the *rosbif* was submitted to the habitual badinage.

'First they buy up all our houses! Now they steal our women!!'

The Pinsons asked us to admire their new bamboo furniture from the CAMIF, which I took to be a ping-pong championship but which turned out to be a mail-order catalogue. The colonial ensemble was guaranteed made by artisans.

'OK,' said Bertrand, 'but what artisans? And where? Adults in Angoulême or minors in Manila?'

While we scoured the catalogue to hunt down illicit delocalizations, a small tray was passed around on which were balanced crunchy *biscottes* precariously spread with lumpfish caviar. The rigidity of the biscottes meant that the garnish fell to the ground at the merest shake or nudge and was immediately gobbled up by the prowling Pampers Brigade. Denis, true to form, threw the delicacies straight on to the floor in order that Gretchen should offer him another a panoramic view of the Black Forest.

An animated conversation ensued about the *bahut*. I crept out into the hall to consult the dictionary on the Ikea shelves. *Bahut*: Why get so worked up about a chest, a trunk or a press? I learnt later it's slang for 'school'. Denis joined me in the kitchen in search of a corkscrew. He put his arm around my shoulder. I was a lucky boy, he told me.

'*Sacré veinard. Putain! Le cul qu'elle a!*' What a great arse!

I assured him I would transmit the compliment to Lou at the first opportunity. We then carried the new fondue kit on to the dining-room table, taking great care not to sprinkle the reclining lumpists with burning oil. At table the extremely lively debate turned around a number of topics: school regulations and the Islamic headscarf, the future of the UMP, which I took to be a mail-order catalogue but which turned out to be the Conservative Party, Slatkine who was in deep depression, and the desire to throw a pupil called Poiccard down a prehistoric hole when the school visited the grottoes at Savennières.

Kirsch – the cherry *eau de vie* – was essential for melting the cheese which would otherwise be in danger of coagulating in the digestive system. I went into the kitchen to fetch a second bottle, Marylène flirtatiously hard on my heels.

'Apparently you don't even know what a *clafoutis* is,' she said, and was about to give me a demonstration when flip-flop Cedric came back for the bread.

'*Ah! Ces Angliches!*' We'll have to lock our women up!

Once back at the table, Béatrice astonished us all.

'I've just bought a caravan,' she announced.

Silence. Her husband Denis gasped. And dropped his fork *not* on purpose. Even the horde of babies stopped stuffing ersatz caviar down their nappies and raised their inquisitive little heads. Béatrice had gone down to the bakers to buy a baguette, had seen the ad at the till, had rung the number and bought it.

'A caravan!' spluttered Denis. 'What the hell are we going to do with a caravan?'

Béatrice unfolded her distress. Living cooped up with a man who drinks and sulks, whose only pastime is throwing crisps on the floor for Bavarian bimbos, is no fun. She wanted to take off for the seaside. To get a change of air. *Changer d'atmosphère*. Denis, who had lost his licence a long time ago, was sardonic.

'And who's going to drive? You ever tried reversing with a caravan?'

Cedric, the perfect host, decided to solve the problem on the spot. He stood. Flip-flop.

'Practice!' he declared. 'Béa needs practice!' And he left to get the Rapido out.

The babies applauded enthusiastically, their sticky clapping hands making the noise of two floppy *tongs* banging together. There was no holding Cedric back. In no time we all found ourselves in the garden moving a pile of wood which had been stacked in front of the garage door. Gretchen was delighted to get down to some real physical activity at last and started singing a peasant folksong as Denis helped her, dropping the odd log in his enthusiasm.

We pushed the caravan to the top of the drive and out on to the road. The orange and green Rapido, with its attractive 1930s corrugated look, was decorated with Star Wars posters; inside, Darth Vader stood guard over a mini-refrigerator. The Picasso reversed into position, headlights ablaze. Cedric stole two cones from a building site up the road.

'*Une compét!*'

A compétition! Serge was over the moon. Caravans were even more exciting than ping pong. To get in training he started doing a series of press-ups, followed by Denis, who made the most of this new vantage-point.

'Here's the rules. You have to back into the parking space marked by the cones. The fastest wins.'

Thanks to generous doses of kirsch we all found this hilarious. Lights went on in the smart apartment blocks around us. Angry voices were heard.

'*Ça suffit. Quand même. On dort!*' If you don't shut up immediately we'll call the police.

Denis cupped his hands to form a megaphone. 'Pay attention. *Ici L'Education Nationale*. We are teachers. Complain, you shall be identified, and your children will never get the *baccalauréat*.'

A heated discussion broke out between the mathematician and the philosopher. Cedric held that, in order to reverse properly, you only had to consult your instinct. Bertrand, *en revanche*, maintained that instinct is irrational and therefore non-consultable. In the meantime Carmen Charpin, who used to spend her holidays down on the farm and could drive a tractor at the age of twelve, had already reversed the Rapido into position. She jumped out of the Picasso waving her victorious arms in the air. Lou Charpin, *agrégée de caravaning*.

It was the turn of the English. I took a swig of kirsch and then, with panache, drove car and caravan skewwiff across the road. Béatrice, inspired by my example, pursued to knock over the cones and drive the Rapido into what until then had been a decorative walnut tree. New protests showered down from the apartment block to the east.

Denis replied, 'This is your children's Biology teacher. We are proceeding with experiments for this year's *baccalauréat*. Stay inside. Do not leave your house in any circumstances!'

To prevent further damage, we retreated to the

pavillon, once again stepping delicately over the army of recumbent babies. Cedric discovered he had lost a *tong*, rapidly recovered by Béatrice, thereby making up for denting the Rapido. A half defrosted *tarte tatin* cooled our ardour.

Sitting around the rattan, non-delocalized coffee-table, I proceeded to give a lesson in the pronunciation of the English 'th', which, as my pupils practised while eating the tart, played havoc with the net curtains. Marylène took me aside, requesting further information as to the precise position of the tongue. Fortunately Cedric whipped his guitar out and I was saved by a group rendition of 'We Shall Not Be Moved'.

On the way home in the Mazda I waxed enthusiastic. 'A great evening!' I declared in my turn.

Lou, in the shadow of the song, was not as impressed. Her colleagues were too much. She'd had enough.

'*J'en ai marre*,' she told me. 'I'm going to change jobs. *Je vais être fleuriste.*'

7

I had to face the fact. Gérard, Lou's ex, was less ex than I had hoped he might have been. She had not concealed this information from me, but nor had she kept me in the picture. I felt moved to broach the subject, endeavouring, as far as possible, to give the impression that I was as cool and unruffled as Aimé Matou's Friesians.

'Lou?'

'Mike?'

I transcribe this opening gambit not, obviously, for its intrinsic interest but in order to illustrate my circumspect approach.

'Your old boyfriend . . .'

'What old boyfriend?'

Diable! How many did she have to choose from?

'You know, the one outside the bathroom in Pont de Ruan.'

'*Alors?* Yes, what about him?' My grammarian is open, direct, frank, earthy, her wit a paintstripper to the acrylic of life.

'Do you still see him?'

'Of course I do. We spent ten years together. I feel responsible.'

This was not the reply I wanted but I listened with affected sympathy. They were going through the delicate period of disengagement, she explained. It was essential that she should discard him gently and with tact. Otherwise he would plunge into the valley of depression – which she called *la sinistrose*.

'Think how you'd have felt,' she said, 'if you'd been an English optician and you'd been dumped by your girlfriend at a fancy-dress party for a Frenchman dressed up as Edith Cresson! You'd hardly have been tickled pick, *non?*'

The parallel called for a little mental agility, but I saw her point.

'For a frog to be abandoned for a *rosbif* . . . tough, non?'

Underneath my dapper academic exterior lurks a marauding Viking, complete with long moustache, chains and a travelling *bahut*, ready to lock up and imprison the booty of my choice – in the present instance the person of Mademoiselle Charpin. I did, however, understand that Gérard must be feeling at least a little Gaulled. Ha-ha.

I decided to carry out my own enquiries.

Mortier Optical – Gérard's business – is situated plum in the middle of the main street of Tours – the rue Nationale. Two glass sliding doors open on to a vast clinically white open space. On the walls, glasses stretch as far as the eye can see – which, given the nature of his clientèle, was perhaps not very far. The frames come in all shapes, colours and sizes, round, square, Buddy Holly, invisible, pink and yellow. They are made of gold, plastic, nylon, and cement for myopic garden gnomes. The *espace* is also occupied by a *coin visagisme*. The art of Julie, Claire and Marie-Ange is explained on a large luminous screen. Each and every face has its own particular shape: rectangular, round, heartshaped or triangular. Basing their calculations on a golden mean established by drawing invisible lines between jaw and cheekbone and cheekbone and forehead, the girls are able to establish your private geometry and thereby harmonize mug and spectacles. Electrifying.

Gérard had inherited his loot from his father who left his mother for a tart and passed away from the excitement. The family house, lurking behind high walls on the Boulevard Béranger, was a carbon copy of the presidential Elysées Palace built in 1937. Gérard was the proud owner of the largest four-wheel drive in the Loire Valley: tank-style tyres carved out of 400 kilos of raw rubber, a 32-horse power engine, guaranteed 40 gallons to the mile in town, tinted windows to prevent people from staring at someone they wouldn't otherwise stare at, armour plating to resist a horde of bison on heat, and an exhaust pipe which, when posed vertically, would not be out of place in the organ loft of Notre Dame. It was the perfect vehicle for travelling the 400 yards between his shop and the lunchtime boiled egg he shared with his mum.

I surveyed the beast with the wonderment of a boy faced with a beached whale. A small dog joined me looking for somewhere to pee. I encouraged him. 'Come on. Good boy. Piss against the whale.' And he obediently cocked his hind leg and urinated on the hubs. 'There's a good dog.'

On the back seat, I noted the latest guide to the swish hotel chain *Relais et Châteaux*, a book on Fiscal Paradises and a CD of Julio Iglesias. At a loose end, I gave the wheels a quick surreptitious kick. The machine leaped into life. *Achtung!!* Aggression!! Lights flashed, the horn sounded and an alarm knifed its way up into the belly of the sky. The dog and I looked surprised at the whale's behaviour. An elderly gentleman, the proprietor of the incontinent canine, joined us to watch the show.

'It's better than the fourteenth of July!' he said gleefully.

I showed him how to do it. As soon as the whale stopped eructating, the merest tap with the foot was enough to set it off again. He left to fetch his friends. At last, something to alleviate the *ennui* of retirement.

Gérard was also a man of adventure. The Paris-Dakar was his goal and the daily boiled-egg race merely a dress rehearsal. In the boot were sun cream, survival rations and a spray to protect you from camel's fleas. He also drove a Quad. On the dashboard I saw a brochure advertising the latest Quadissimo 500cc – a four-wheel motorbike, the latest gadget for smart, sensation-seeking urbanites. The machine looked like a helium-inflated ladybird.

Gérard belonged to a racing club which organized rallies in the domains of the châteaux de la Loire. In a few days' time, the twelve hours of Ussé would unleash a flock of Formula One ladybirds in the woods of the Sleeping Beauty who, on this particular occasion, was going to find it difficult to nod off. Cher Gérard would be speeding along country tracks astride his souped-up mini-tractor, slaloming around badgers at 80 kilometres an hour, giving heart-attacks to moles. *Quel pied!* What fun!

Lou's disengagement strategy apparently involved lending a helping hand to the intrepid optician. She explained the adventure. What was dangerous in daylight, she said, became literally deadly at night. I immediately saw the advantage of the event and, always a good sport, offered to muck in.

We were to supply the back-up support. A tent erected in a clearing would serve as the pitstop. Every two laps, our Schumacher of the night would pull in for refuelling, vitamins, massage and soup. Lou sent me out to do some preparatory shopping. I felt a wimp, buying fruit bars for my rival and, in amongst the goodies, I slipped a few sugar-free chocolates. With any luck he'd eat them without looking at the wrapper, run out of energy and drive into a tree. Life is a jungle. Every man to himself. *Quad erat demonstrandum*.

The gruelling race was to start at sunset and finish at dawn. Lou and I left for the woods in the early evening, with her driving Gérard's tank, full of gear. I was impressed by the Concorde-style dashboard.

'Stop playing with the controls, Michael. You'll break something!'

'*Désolé . . .*' And I managed to close the roof just too late to prevent the upholstery being squirted with anti-camel-flea gunge.

The pitstop was an arbour of verdant green dappled in the light of the setting sun. But this was no time for poetry. The tent had to be erected, post haste! In the distance we could hear the ladybirds snarling and revving up on their starting blocks. The tent was packed in a hessian bag. Lou installed the gas ring and bottle while I took care of the erection. I shook the bag and the little metal skewers fell out into the grass.

'*Les sardines. Attention!*' shouted Lou.

Take care of the sardines? I rummaged through the grocery bag.

'What the hell are you doing?' she demanded.

'I can't find them.'

'Can't find the what?'

'The sardines.'

'*Pas les sardines, Mike. Les* sardines.'

Clear as mud.

'Look. There – on the ground.'

How was I to know that a skewer is a *sardine* in French? Skewers in olive oil? And there they were, shining in the shadowy tall grass, looking more like glow worms than fish. On hand and knees I rapidly picked them up. Fangio would be on us in no time.

I had never been a Boy Scout. I could have been, since I found the uniform attractive and was partial to soft felt hats but, at that particular time of my life – indeed, ever since – I have been more interested in girls than in knots. Unfortunately, a certain knowledge of young ladies, unlike Scouting, does not help put up tents.

In the bottom of the tent bag was an instruction booklet explaining how to erect the thing in sixteen languages. It would not stay open in the wind and I reconciled myself to working in Estonian. Like the cosmos or an unsuccessful omelette, the vast canvas sheet seemed to have neither beginning nor end. I folded it and unfolded it, desperately looking for shape. In vain. In order to discover its flaps and doors, I decided to get inside it and suspend the whole lot from my head, using my body as a tentpole, It was at that moment that Lou looked up from the soup. She was taken aback by the army surplus ghost floundering in front of her.

'Mike! *Fais pas le con.* Give it to me. You don't look like the world's greatest handyman.'

She took the omelette in hand while I stood back and admired her. I had never realized that erecting a tent could be such an erotic activity. It struck me: what if all this was a test? Would I be able to assemble an Ikea wardrobe? The bunk beds for the twins?

'Dad! I'm twelve. When's my cot going to be ready?'

Mr Adventure arrived for the first pitstop, looking, with his goggles and scarf, like Biggles astride a motorized bidet. After an hour and ten minutes at 60 kilometres an hour along dirt tracks, his undercarriage must have been in terrible nick but I chose not to pursue the point. Lou contented herself with massaging the back of his neck. One sigh of pleasure and I would paint his goggles black. We stuffed his face with some dried fruit – and good riddance. At last we were alone.

I was left to inflate the mattress while Lou disappeared into the undergrowth with a torch looking for kindling wood. Inflation was my kind of activity. I'd always been a dab hand with a pump. In no time at all the rubber tubes were as taut and firm as a series of arrogant sausages. But Lou had other things in mind than to admire my pumping. She emerged from the woods with the bottom of her pullover rolled up into a makeshift basket.

'*C'est fou!*' Nestled in the woolly cradle were a collection of multi-coloured mushrooms. 'What a find. *Cêpes, bolets, girolles, chanterelles, tompettes de la mort.*'

She was ecstatic. I was less so. 'Trumpets of death?!' I echoed.

Lou was in no mood for listening. She wanted me to get out the frying pan so she could feed me pleasures, the like of which I had never tasted before.

And would never taste again? I could already see the headlines: 'Rally of death. Academic and his muse found inert in clearing. A great literary career felled by a mushroom.'

'Are you quite sure that they are safe to eat?'

'Quelle poule mouillée!'

A wet hen? Hang on a minute. There's nothing wet-henish about avoiding a painful death by poisoning. I've often looked at the mushroom maps in the windows of pharmacies. You have to be very, very careful.

'There's so little difference between the edible and the—' I began defensively, but Lou cut me off.

'You don't know what you're talking about. I am French. My father taught me. It's in my blood.'

There's the rub: it was soon going to be in mine as well. The argument was clearly finished because Lou had already set about scraping the mushrooms and tossing them in the frying pan so that they would shed excess dew and water.

'Pass the butter,' she said briskly.

One, of course, inevitably finds in the pitstop equipment of every professional French racing driver, garlic, salt, pepper and butter.

'And Chernobyl?' I enquired. And radioactive fall-out?

'Don't be so wet.'

At least we'll die together.

A few minutes later: *'Divin, non?'*

'Absolutely . . . Yes . . . delicious.'

'Smile.'

When Gérard skidded in for his second stop, this time there was a difference. Who did we see sitting on the pillion clutching on to the optician's leather jacket for dear life, his eyes reddened from peering into the speeding blackness? Dylan. Yes, *le keum* in person. What a sly move. Gérard had doubtless rung and proposed a new experience. 'Forget Shakespeare. Throw *Lear* to the winds. Come and prove yourself a man.' *À la guerre comme à la guerre.* All is fair in love and war. Gérard was pursuing the same strategy as me. Get the family in your pocket! Bravo, Gérard. One to you, clever sod.

It started to rain and we slipped inside the tent. Lou sat on my deftly inflated mattress and undid her hair. As the black curls tumbled down her back, I felt an immediate and urgent desire to sink my face into this warm silky mass. I looked at her back and a word rose unexpectedly from the depths of my unconscious. That word was *croupe*. Now I was not displeased that my unconscious could, in a tent, discharge unusual French words. I'd read it first at school in the poems of Charles Baudelaire and had shelved it in a distant drawer. *Croupe* from the German *Kruppe* – croup, crupper, rump, buttocks. This is not the kind of word that you can just slip into a conversation without people noticing. 'I say, that's a jolly nice croup,' would cause a rumpus. I was, therefore, delighted at last to have an opportunity of putting it to some use.

'*Lou,*' I said, '*tu as une croupe magnifique.*'

'*Une magnifique quoi??*' Clearly she had not been expecting the compliment. While her ex risked coming a cropper deep in the ancestral woods, her present lover started waxing lyrical about her crupper. She looked at me and said in a scolding tone, 'If I have understood correctly, we are here to man the pit – OK? Gérard is at this moment fighting off depression on his Quad, and all you can do is to prattle on about *ma croupe*?'

I was chastened and put the word hastily back in its box. At that precise moment a frog croaked.

'*Beurk!*'

Lou had once told me that she couldn't stand slimy creatures. Then why go out with Gérard in the first place? At last, however, a weakness. *Enfin* I could protect her from creepy crawlies. I put a kindly arm around her and stretched her out on the taut Lilo. The croaking grew in intensity as the rain poured down. She shivered. A whole slimy choir began to croak its chorus around the tent. Lou shuddered.

'We must get a little sleep,' she said, and yawned. A couple of minutes late, she had drifted off. My stomach began to make odd noises. I prodded my abdomen, searching for telltale signs of death. A few minutes later I drifted off myself, only to wake up with a start. Where was I? I looked at my watch. In ten minutes Gérard would be back. I was just about to wake Lou up when I stopped, horrified. There, on her inflated pillow was a squat, black shape. An evil frog – in this instance not the optician – must have crept into the tent, squeezing its way passed the sardines I'd left on sentry duty outside.

What was I to do? Her sleeping head was turned frogwise. If I woke her up, she'd open her eyes, scream with horror and the viscous thing would jump down her throat. It was essential that she remained still. But I had no particular desire to touch the slimy beast myself. I very cautiously reached out to get my hands on the towel we had been using to give Fangio a rubdown. My hands finally touched the spongy material in the dark. With the deft movement of a born cricketer, I threw the towel over the beast.

Lou woke up with a start.

'*Quoi?* What the . . .? What's going on?'

I whispered a swift warning. 'Whatever you do, don't move.' With another coordinated, virile movement of arm and wrist, I grabbed the spongy bundle and tossed towel and reptile out of the tent.

There was a sudden and unexpected noise. *Psssssssssss . . .*

'What's happening!' Lou demanded.

'There was a frog on your pillow,' I began to explain. *Psssssssssss . . .*

'I wrapped it in the towel and threw it outside.' *Psssssssssss . . .*

'Mike!'

What was wrong now?

'That wasn't a frog on my pillow.'

'What was it?'

'That was the stopper of my Lilo.'

Psssssssssss . . .

She was right. Slowly but inexorably, she and the mattress were going down.

I waited for Lou to put the boot in, to criticise my deepseated Anglo-Saxon imbecility, to tell me that in *Les Liaisons dangereuses* Valmont never deflated the Lilo of Madame de Meurteuil. But I was wrong. She laughed. She laughed until the tears ran down her cheeks. Then she took me in the arms.

'*T'es fou,*' she said. '*T'es impossible! Ah! Vous, les Anglais . . .*'

Seduce an *agrégée de grammaire*? Simple. All you need is a frog and a Lilo. Nothing to it. *Fastoche.* Easy as falling off a mattress.

8

The only competition which was of any real interest to Mortier and myself was the Prix Charpin. Gérard had just played a dirty trick with Dylan. I decided to advance on the granny front. Emmeline, according to my sources, didn't think much of the Mortier family. Her late husband Léon had come home from the Palais Optical wearing a pair of new half-moon specs which his wife considered to be bourgeois, reactionary, tight-arsed and prissy. Emmeline, in her nineties, was pretty rock 'n' roll.

For *La Toussaint* I launched my special charm offensive.

All Saints' Day, when the French salute their dearly departed by smothering gravestones in geraniums, was very busy. At Toison the cemetery became a hive of activity. Cracks were Polyfilla-ed, slabs cleaned and weeded, Roundup sprayed in the alleys, statues given a yearly springclean. Monsieur Dumas had come up with the idea of a windscreen-wiper for headstones – the tombwiper. Last year, Madame Santon, whose sight was failing, had placed a wreath from Atac costing 36 Euros on the tomb of a Belgian who had died of a heart-attack during a wet T-shirt evening at the Club Gliss in Noizy. A grave mistake.

Tradition has it that on 1 November, families have a communal lunch before all trooping off red-faced down to the cemetery. Windows never seen open before, bang in the wind to air the spare room. The son of Henri, who is in his second year at the Sorbonne studying Archaeology, was bringing his new Parisian girlfriend who had apparently never seen a cow. Nestor the baker's son, who had a shoe shop in Lille, would soon arrive with his annual pun: *'J'ai mis mes pompes funèbres.' Les pompes funèbres* means the undertaker's. *Pompes* is also slang for shoes. This joke took me three weeks to fathom, by which time it was a bit late to laugh.

Marcellin of the N'Garage, was in the depths of despair. Louis, the husband of Monique, his bus-driving muse, was home from his oil rig for six days and seven nights. The school was on holiday. Deprived of the merest glimpse of Monique, Marcellin went to stay with his cousin in Toulouse to drown his sorrows in *cassoulet*.

Such was the activity in the Charpin family that there was no one to accompany Emmeline to the cemetery. To be precise, Sylvie was ready and willing but Emmeline turned her down. She found her morbid. Sylvie would prepare tapes of the favourite music of the dearly departed and would go round the tombs laying musical wreaths – a military band on one and the Greatest Hits of the World of the Accordion on the other. A pain.

For fear that Gérard might pipe up, step in and take her round on his Quad like the late Queen Mother on her golf buggy, I volunteered. Emmeline was ninety-six, and, in her own words, 'an unconscionable time going'. There had been many alerts. Her vision was no longer as good as it had been and she would mistake the TV remote control for the Homecare Alert Device.

Every time she changed channels, she signalled an attack. Real alerts there had been. Her exaggerated taste for a Martini-like apéritif called Ambassadeur and her avowed passion for Boursin cheese with chives and garlic created a dubious cocktail in her digestive system which gave rise to what she would refer to as her 'trips'. At Homecare they called her Granny Woodstock.

Emmeline, chic and alert, her eyes and her hair the same intense blue, opened the door of the small flat where she still lived alone. She was ready and I was late. She immediately stepped into and completely filled the lift and I had to run downstairs to keep up both with her and the conversation.

Loading an elegant ninety-six year old into a compact Mazda was no easy business. It would have been more practical via the hatchback but it was unthinkable to treat an empress like a washing-machine. Finally we made it, a complex ballet of thighs, knees and walking sticks. Emmeline had her opinion. I should have bought a Renault, she complained. Japanese cars were designed for Japanese grannies.

However, the installation process was no drain on her energies. She didn't think much of the driving skills of her compatriots, and let them know as much.

'Get your finger out! *L'andouille!*' You prat! Then, giving a magisterial *bras d'honneur*, '*Branleur!*' Wanker!

The drivers in question accelerating out of trouble to escape the wrath of the gesticulating granny.

On arriving at the cemetery, Emmeline flirted with the idea of being carted around in the municipal wheelbarrow, but in the end decided to do the rounds on my arm.

'It's not as if we had to hurry', she said comfortably.
'They're all dead.'

She knew everybody. It was like walking into a
cocktail party where all the guests were horizontal.
Emmeline introduced me to her friends with their wonderful old-world names – Bertille, Eugénie, Donatienne.

'Quite a girl, *she* was', this about Donatienne. 'A
bum and a half on her, I can tell you.'

What most attracted her attention was the decorative
masonry: exterminating angels with limestone trumpets
straight out of *Don Giovanni*, huge solid blocks of
concrete just waiting for the hand of Dracula to lift
them up and – much in vogue – vast black slabs of
marble. I was tempted to take my felt pen and inscribe
85% cocoa on them but resisted.

Emmeline was dismissive. 'A load of crap.' The place
lacked imagination, she said, pointing at the grave of a
charcutier from Montlouis, who was buried under
a run-of-the-mill archangel. Couldn't they have come
up with something more appropriate, like a pink pig, or
a marble pork chop?

We arrived at our destination – the plot where Léon,
her husband with the half-moon glasses, was buried.
Emmeline for once approved. Léon had a simple head-
stone on which was engraved, as if on the tympanum of
an Italianate church, the crest of his profession. He had
been an Inspector in the *Education Nationale*.

'Now that's what I call class,' observed Emmeline.

The only problem. There was no room at the inn.

Four coffins stacked vertically one upon the other
was all the municipality would allow. She could have
sought permission to take one out and incinerate the
occupant but Emmeline had no desire to gatecrash. A
nagging worry remained. How was she to disappear in

style? What the hell could they put on *her* gravestone?

Leaning on her two walking sticks, Emmeline told me the terrible story of a friend of hers. Edwige, like Emmeline, had hithered and dithered. She couldn't make her mind up what she wanted and finally left things too late. She was cremated while her family tried to sort the matter out. In the meantime her ashes were stored in an urn in the garden shed. There was a burglary and they were nicked along with the mower. With the result that – before being recovered by the police in Vierzon – she spent two years in the boot of an Opel Astra.

'Can you imagine! In a bloody Opel?'

I reloaded Emmeline in the Mazda and headed off home. Her flat was in a 1960s five-storey building next to the municipal swimming pool. Through the open window, filtered by the luxurious bio-high geraniums, came the excited cries of wet children and, when the breeze was from the west, the acrid smell of chlorine. On the large ornate *buffet* or sideboard which took up at least half of the living space of her salon, stood a framed photograph of Léon in his uniform as *inspecteur d'académie*; next to him was an autographed portrait of Patrice Laffont, who was the presenter of a programme called *Les Chiffres et Les lettres*, a quiz game which kept Emmeline's mind alive and alert under the blue rinse.

The afternoon had been a success, and I was of the opinion that I had *damé le pion* of Gérard Mortier – that I had wiped my rival off the emotional chessboard. There was no question, however, of slipping quietly and triumphantly away. Emmeline was already removing the flowery plastic tablecloth from the imitation Louis XIII table.

'*Une petite partie,*' she told me. It was a statement,

not a question. A Scrabble box was produced from the *buffet*.

'No, actually, if you don't mind, I've got an important . . .' I blustered, but it was no use. Emmeline, in principle, couldn't hear and wouldn't listen. A bottle of sticky Ambassadeur made its appearance on the table, accompanied by a tin box carrying the effigy of President Georges Pompidou with his bushy eyebrows. She kept her nibbles in this. She dealt me a slug.

'Up yours,' she toasted, and screwed a Craven A into her tortoiseshell cigarette-holder, at the same time jumbling the ivory letters in the green felt bag.

'*Une petite partie . . . internationale,*' she added, then arranged her letters on the stand and passed me the bag. 'Shoot.'

There was no point in protesting. In any event, I told myself, a game of Scrabble could only last – what? – half an hour at the most. Fool. Three hours later, battered and bewildered, I emerged shattered and totally humiliated. This, I was to learn, was the state in which Emmeline would leave all her fellow Scrabblers. The lady from upstairs, who loathed games, used to lend her husband until the state of nervous exhaustion in which Emmeline returned him proved even too much for Lexomyl. Emmeline knew the rules off by heart and was an unbeatable mistress of the obscure and arcane: Afghan swearwords, Chinese tombstones, Wu, Xhosa, wok, zeugma – you name it, she knew it.

'Vollington. Vollington boot.'

'Actually, Emmeline, we – that is, normally – tend to say Wellington. Welllington boot.'

'*Normalement*? *Et anormalement*? Vollington. *C'est anglais.*' She was very persuasive.

'But I am English, Emmeline.'

'*On s'en fout!*' So what!

Before leaving, in a desperate last-minute attempt to regain a few grammes of my lost status, I told her about a quaint new burial practice in Britain: the firework funeral. Not knowing what was to be done with their ashes, a good number of Brits have had recourse to pyrotechnics. Instead of running the risk of ending up in an urn in an Opel, they have entrusted their remains to a firework expert. Mixed with a reasonable amount of gunpowder, the ashes are stuffed in one or more skyrockets, and if so wished, the dearly departed can bid farewell in one mighty and rather glorious tableau. A horseracing punter in a reconstitution of Beecher's Brook. A curry lover in a tableau of the Taj Mahal. Emmeline, I suggested, could shuffle off her mortal coil with a fiery and multi-coloured tableau of a bottle of Ambassadeur.

There was a silence. Her look turned me into St Sebastian, pierced by darts. I could now leave. She thought I was mad.

'*Dingue,*' she muttered darkly. '*Ils sont complètement dingues, ces rosbifs.*'

0 out of 10 again.

Mission a write-off.

9

Qui est Lou? Who exactly is Lou Charpin?

Her sister gave me an opportunity to crack the mystery. Sylvie, herself, was like the amoeba, the single nucleus protozoa that rapidly reproduces and moves around thanks to its pseudo pods – the only difference being that Sylvie moved around in a Twingo and had never reproduced. A nucleus she certainly did have, however. Hers was the *famille Charpin*. She would cry bitter tears whenever dissension loomed – the *clafoutis* row had disturbed her inner peace for ten days – and turn to the bottle to drown her sorrows. Lou was afraid she was going to end up with neurosis of the liver.

PA to the managing director of a factory in the industrial zone of Joué les Tours which made aluminium trays – *des barquettes* – for freezer storing, Sylvie was an ardent prophet of the company's wares. Competition from the Far East was fierce, but the average Korean sole was shorter than the French sole. To fit local fish in an Asian *barquette* involved folding and contortion. If you didn't want to bend your bass, then buy Bisson.

Rumour had it that Sylvie was having an affair with Pierre-Louis Bisson, the owner, whose name was brandished across the packaging featuring a stylized but contented cod. They and the family were of great discretion. It was Mum's the Word. *Motus et bouche cousue.*

Sylvie invited me to meet Edouard, their uncle, a gentleman who had once had a position of responsibility in the local hierarchy of the EDF – the national French electricity company. Edouard had a problem, *pauvre chou*. She didn't let on what the poor cabbage's hang-up was, but his niece Lou was the apple of his eye.

'Dress for summer,' Sylvie warned me, before we went to visit. '*Chez Edouard*, it's ninety degrees in the shade.'

In France, employees of EDF get free energy. You only have to walk around a small French town at night. The house with an electric gate, a fountain in the garden, three alarms and a year-round illuminated Rudolf and sleigh, will be the local EDF representative flaunting his kilowatts.

Wearing Bermudas, I parked the Mazda under a baby lime tree in front of the Résidence Royale Bord de Loire, and climbed the imitation marble staircase lit by wrought-iron wall-brackets in the shape of medieval banners. By the time I reached his apartment on the third floor, I was already sweating. Sylvie, dressed for the beach, opened the door and took me into the salon.

'*Je te présente Michael, un ami de Lou.*'

I was none too happy with the noun *ami*, friend. *Petit ami*, boyfriend, would have been preferable but I couldn't ask for too much too soon. And what about the indefinite article – *un ami*. Was I merely *un* amongst *plusieurs*? Did they troop up the stairs week after week for the great meltdown?

'*Ah, la petite Lou . . . Un sacré numéro!*'

Edouard was a bachelor with a penchant for cats and a singer of light opera called Luis Mariano, a man with a voice as smooth as Brylcreem. Dapper in cravat and cardigan, Edouard had once been in love with the daughter of an affluent ironmonger from Blois, but she had been promised to another. He had remained ever faithful to her memory, refusing temptation, using up his energy (and that of the EDF) by cultivating his melancholy.

I moved gingerly into the furnace. Everything was melting. The radiators, straight out of a Dali painting, were going rapidly soft, two fluorescent begonias were burned at the stake, three fat cats had melted into the cushions of the canapé while a pouf, looking like a large Livarot cheese, was dripping into the thick pile carpet.

The flat smelled fusty, a suffocating atmosphere made up of the condensed steam emitted by several years of leek soup, dried flowers, old cat food, Madeira cake, superannuated peanuts, and the farts of tropical fish in the exotic tank whose constant flatulence could be seen bubbling its way to the surface under the lazy eye of the melting felines.

On an embroidered tablecloth with matching napkins, Edouard had laid ready three Limoges china cups and a cake-dish depicting what looked like a team of Chinamen playing bowls. In place of tea, however, he had had the bright idea of serving a delicious mellow *quart de chaumes* from Anjou, a perfect wine for tea, which cooled the innards and delayed the bodily combustion threatened by the central heating. He started the conversation.

'Yesterday, what did I eat? Yesterday, I started the day with a bowl of coffee and two *biscottes*. No, two and half. With butter and apricot jam. Just a minute. Yesterday was Thursday. No, it was three. Three *biscottes*.'

Now I do have a thing about *biscottes*. *Biscottes* are

the extremely disappointing French answer to toast. Here our mighty culinary neighbours have gone off the rails. *Biscottes* are more like rusks than bread, both brittle and crumbly. You push your knife down on a *biscotte* to spread the butter and the bloody thing breaks in half, causing the jam to fall in a lump on your recently cleaned and nicely pressed trousers. In *Baisers volés* (Truffaut, 1968) Antoine Doinel does prove that a *biscotte* can be made solid by placing a second *biscotte* under the first, thereby providing a firm base. This, I maintain, is a dirty trick, obliging the consumer, in an attempt to save his trousers, to buy twice the number of *biscottes* he would normally want, lumbering his larder with unwanted packets of foundation rusks. Yes, I did have things to say about *biscottes*, but I didn't get the chance. Edouard's conversation was a nonstop stream of consciousness, a little on the nutty side of bonkers.

'At eleven o'clock I had a banana . . .' he continued. 'For lunch, *rillettes, bifteck haché*, fresh green beans, Camembert and a yoghurt. A cup of chocolate and a *tartine* at four-thirty. In the evening, soup, an artichoke and another piece of Camembert.'

The French rightly pride themselves on their art of conversation. From the salons of Louis XIV to the literary cafés of the Boulevard St Germain, the nation has long developed the art of chattering. Uncle Edouard was rather letting the side down. He sounded more like a weirdo straight out of a play by Ionesco. Sylvie, to my surprise, was delighted by his badinage.

'I do think, *cher Edouard*,' she cooed, 'that you may have forgotten an essential.'

Edouard looked puzzled and then delighted. And the two of them in unison chanted the missing ingredient.

'*Le Crunch! Le Crunch!*'

Had they fallen out of their mutual trees? *Biscottes*, yes, bananas *peut-être*, but Le Crunch *certainement pas*. But I didn't have time to express my consternation. Edouard, turning his back on the tea party, was already standing engrossed at the window. There was a long silence. Then:

'There are exactly two hundred and thirty-two swallows perched on the telegraph wire,' he told us.

By now, my mind was reeling, and not only from the tropical temperature. Menus, Crunch, now birds . . . When Edouard left to fetch a *bavaroise glacée* (the cold Bavarian woman turned out to be a cake) from the kitchen, Sylvie, sotto voce, explained it all to me. Edouard was frightened of losing his marbles. To stop the rot setting in, he would grab any chance to keep his neurones on their toes.

'Tell Michael all about Lou, Edouard,' she suggested.

Chouette! Great! I sat back and opened a mental notebook.

'Well,' he began, 'Lou weighed 3.2 kilos at birth.'

Tiens! You don't say.

'She won her first swimming certificate for breast-stroke at the age of nine. She had a passion for *bigorneaux* – winkles.' In 1989 on the Ile de Ré she apparently came home with a bag containing 2.4 kilos of the little buggers.

Electrifying.

'Her first flat was at 17, rue des Halles. The lease was signed on 25 September. Rent 260 francs a month, *charges comprises*. Two windows. Kitchenette.'

And so on for the next ten minutes, until Sylvie decided he had passed the test and got up to fetch a ball to test his reflexes. Meanwhile I went for a stroll around the apartment to mull over my statistics, and ended up in the enclosed greenhouse veranda where Edouard grew his houseplants and herbs. And stopped, shocked. Only once before in my life had I stumbled on a similar plantation – in the wardrobe of a friend in Paris.* But never in full view, in broad daylight. Each flower pot had been scrupulously named: thyme, rosemary, mint, coriander. But who did they think they were going to fool? On Edouard's balcony was a flourishing dope patch. Wall-to-wall hash, or shit as the French so poetically call it.

What was he up to? Why was there so much grass in his garden?!

Sylvie called me. He musn't get tired. It was time to go.

Once outside again, we looked up and Edouard knocked on the window to wave us goodbye. There he was, the Pedro Escobar of Tours Sud, standing proudly on his balcony surrounded by enough dope to net him a mint and put him inside for twenty years.

Bizarre, bizarre.

* See *An Englishman in Paris* (Pocket Books, 2003).

10

Eroticism is an exacting sport.

It all began with offal. I was shopping in the Atac supermarket when a very handsome kidney eyed me from the bottom of its *barquette*. Now at my age, with my experience of life, I should have known better than to heed the siren song of a tarty kidney. Attractive offal can be resisted in a number of ways – by switching one's gaze in the opposite direction or by paying especial attention to the nearby shelf of household cleansing products. But I didn't. Like a fool I just stood there ogling the kidney. Not, as I have intimated, that this was a run-of-the-mill kidney. Pale, pink, lustrous, this one was a real turn-on.

I plumped not to resist temptation and slipped the object of my desire into the trolley, concealing it under a packet of filo pastry with which I intended to make something flash like goat's cheese and parsley Paradise Packets. *Ni vu ni connu*. Or so I thought.

'*Maï-quel!*' Ariane Tricot's sultry voice pulled me up short.

'*Quel plaisir!*'

Ariane was the sophisticated wife of Brice Tricot, the Cultural Attaché of Loches. Ever since she had rolled me a skate or a shovel – *rouler un patin* or *rouler une pelle* are two variants of French kiss – at a firework party at the Château de la Touche, her proximity had instilled a mixture of panic and desire.

'*Maï-quel . . .*'

Her voice had the same effect as the kidney. I tried the same antidote, staring desperately in the direction of Omo and Ajax.

'*Alors? Raconte. On ne se voit plus.* We never see each other! *Quoi de neuf?* What's new?'

I was her ex-English teacher and she always spoke in subtitles. She pursued me remorselessly.

'But you look embarrassed, *Maï-quel*! What have you been doing? *Il y a anguille sous roche?* Something is amiss? Zere is an eel under ze rocks?'

More a question of a kidney under the pastry. I blushingly blurted out in an English manner that in fact, yes, now she came to mention it, funny that but well gosh yes, I actually had a new girlfriend.

'*Mais je sais!!*'

How did she know?

'*Un professeur! Comme c'est excitant!*'

I sensed she was taking the mickey. Her eyes darted coals of fire in my direction.

'*Il faut que tu me la présentes,*' she added, and then huffed off as if to say, 'No replacement for *me* is possible . . . *Maï-quel.*'

Lou's flat is situated on the Place des Halles, above the florists Le Bouquet de Daphné. Daphné, an attractive bunch herself, was contemplating early retirement and Lou, tired of the rigours of the *Education Nationale*, was toying with the idea of stepping into her clogs. I broodily carried shopping – including an extremely handsome cucumber – back to Lou's apartment.

Cucumbers are dangerous territory, and their preparation a bone of contention. Lou, for instance, half-peels in strips, then cuts them up and sprinkles the slices with sea salt an hour before serving, in order for the cucumber to *dégorger* – get rid of excess water. The intention to concentrate the cucumberliness of the cucumber is laudable, but the problem is that it loses its crunchiness in the process. My slices are, admitted, watery but they are crisp. Lou's are tasteful but floppy. Fortunately, this difference, albeit profound, had not yet undermined the edifice of our affection.

The kidney posed another problem. Like the eye in the tomb of Cain in Victor Hugo's poem 'La Conscience', it wouldn't stop looking at me. As I wriggled with guilt, Lou's footsteps sounded on the rickety stairs. The door opened and the *agrégée* entered the flat, kicked off her shoes, came up behind me and very sensually enveloped me in her arms.

At this juncture the author pauses and downs his pen. A doubt crosses his brow, deepening the furrows like those of a distant ploughed field. Should he continue? Or should he rather, as in the prudish cinema of the 1950s, displace the centre of attention, moving the camera sideways to allow the spectator to contemplate tropical fish frolicking in a decorative tank while the lovers, locked in a torrid embrace, get on with the job offscreen?

I think not.

Sex with a partner with whom you do not share the same tongue can be a tricky business. The enterprise, an experiment in applied ethnology, deserves to be chronicled. The following is not intended to be voyeuristic or exhibitionist. The account has been constructed to light the path of other intrepid explorers who seek to venture into the more uncharted territories of love.

Preparation is essential. A certain mastery of anatomical vocabulary will come in handy. In moments of intensity, you won't want to find yourself at a loss as to where to go, or what to grab. At the toss of a hat you must be ready to identify *le sternum*, to displace *le sacrum*, or to wiggle *le coccyx*. What is more, to avoid getting bogged down in the endless repetition of *ma chérie*, you must learn to branch out into the culinary. *Mon chou* – my cabbage – is an acceptable variant. As is *mon cornichon doré* – my golden gherkin. Do *not* improvise.

'You look delicious this evening, *ma tartiflette*,' evoked great scorn.

The names of cuddly animals can be put to good use: *mon chaton* – my kitten; *ma gazelle* – same word; *ma biche* – my doe; *ma poule* – my hen (be careful with this one as it can also mean 'harlot' as does 'morue' – cod); and *mon lapin* – my rabbit – can be used parsimoniously. *Ma chienne* – my bitch – and *ma gerboise* – my gerbil – misfired completely. Language is a minefield.

The Brits tend to suffer from an inferiority complex. Do the French do it differently? Do they do things we don't do? If so, who told them? Where did they learn? Are there evening classes?

I decided to take the bull by the horns and to record the soft porn late-night movie on Sunday evening on the M6 Channel. Much of *Le Technicien de surface* (the politically correct term for a cleaner but a pun on the job of Jean-Claude, the male lead, who was a dermatologist and a *chaud lapin* – a hot rabbit i.e. a womanizer) took place in the broom cupboard. Mado, the voluptuous cleaning lady, a dab hand in keeping everything spick and span, was mad about her employer. In the final scene their strenuous encounter created havoc amongst the cleaning equipment. The brushes, brooms, bin bags and plastic bottles went all over the shop. Clearly the classic venues – bedrooms, boudoirs, luxury hotels – no longer had any wind in their sails – *n'avait plus le vent en poupe*.

I was careful to copy down the dialogue. Mado, the head of her lover deeply ensconced in her bosom, uttered a sentence of such Racinian intensity that it has remained with me ever since:

'*Mords-moi, Jean-Claude.*' The translation, 'Bite me, Jean-Claude,' in no way does justice to the erotic poetry of the invitation.

I was thus prepared but nervous when Lou took me from behind as I prepared my *hors-d'oeuvres*. The kitchen must be her preferred erotic territory. If so, jolly good. Better than a broom cupboard, if you ask me – more airy and less prickly. She enticed me down on to the floor and I followed suit, carelessly knocking a few ingredients off the worktop as I slid to her side. I was quick to point out how delightful this all was.

'Did you know, *mon amour*,' she breathed, 'that the word *délice* is masculine in the singular and feminine in the plural?'

'Good heavens, no I—'

'We say *des délices infini-e-s*'.'

'How extraordinary! I must fetch my vocabulary book. I've left it . . .'

'*Répète.*'

And I repeated my lesson, my breathing somewhat impaired by the position of my *sternum*.

'Same thing for the word *amour*. We say *un amour fervent* but *des belles amours*.'

Fascinating how an *agrégée* functions. Head and heart seem independent.

'In French, the masculine and the feminine are often confused . . .' she whispered.

I was about to point out that this is a common English failing when she nibbled my earlobe and I began to lose command of my lexical abilities. Not so Lou.

'There is even doubt as to the gender of *pample-mousse*. It is feminine for the Académie Française, but masculine for the *Dictionnaire Littré*.'

At this particular stage of the proceedings I could no longer give a fart for the sex of fruit. Lou began to cuddle closer and then stopped. An expression of delight and worry crossed her face.

'Mike!'

'What had I done? And then I remembered. Shit. She'd rolled on the cucumber. In order to dispel any misunderstanding, I decided to bring out the big guns. I kissed her, urgently, deeply, passionately. I knew this was the moment. I pulled back, looked at her with intensity, and then whispered in her ear.

'*Mords-moi, Jean-Claude.*'

Quel con! I had forgotten to omit the vocative. Lou looked at me in surprise as if she'd rolled on a second cucumber. Was it true what they'd told her about the English?

There was still, it was clear, work to be done.

Il y a du pain sur la planche.

11

Just before Christmas a phone call from Thierry, the husband of Lou's younger sister Cécile, who had married the first suitor to knock at the door for fear that he would be the last. Thierry desperately wanted a son. So far, they had four daughters. The quest continued.

One evening, as we were walking in the countryside, a whiff of an industrial pig farm wafting around our nostrils, Lou evoked her brother-in-law.

'He's turned Cécile into *une poule pondeuse* – a brood hen. We used to do crazy things together. No more. It's tragic. Make her laugh, Mike.'

Message received. When Thierry phoned I was primed.

'*J'ai besoin d'un Anglais,*' he began, then added, laughing at his own joke, 'Nabody's porfect.'

The quip 'nobody's perfect' – the last line of *Some Like It Hot* – is the reply you inevitably get when you tell a Frenchman that you're English. The routine goes like this:

'*Je suis Anglais,*' you say, as if the accent, the tweeds and the numberplates were not a sufficient giveaway. At which your interlocutor smiles, winks, nudges and says: 'Nobidies pirfock,' in one of its many phonetic disguises.

You must then dutifully smile as if this is the first

time you have heard the joke, instead of putting your finger up their nose.

Thierry spelled out his scheme. He had stumbled on a real gem not far from Toison – a fantastic little house that he could snap up for a song – and he wanted my advice. He and the family would stop by and pick me up on Sunday.

Squat and balding, looking like a pear in a hurry, Dr Thierry was an amateur estate agent. Expert in human arteries, he had recently decided to instal an automatic watering system, in the garden of his townhouse in Tours. Louis XIV had designed the irrigation channels at Versailles by copying charts illustrating the circulation of the blood. If a seventeenth-century King had pulled this off, why not a twenty-first-century medic? Job done, he left for a varicose-vein rally in Prague while Cécile took the girls off for a few days of sea air in La Baule. When they returned, disaster. A tropical jungle on the left, the Gobi Desert on the right. An expensive mistake. Thierry lost several cubic metres of costly tapwater and several clients, taken aback at his circulatory incompetence.

On Sunday morning, he arrived at the house in a cloud of dust and a Porsche. Cecile and the girls would be following in an old Renault Espace, which he referred to as *la bétaillière à catho* – the Catholic cattle-wagon. He immediately walked into the kitchen without being invited, opened the box of cakes I had bought for the children and ate three *religieuses*, wiping the excess cream off on to his hair like Brylcreem.

'You wouldn't by any chance have *une petite gnôle*?' he asked.

My eyes lit up. At last a chance not only to get rid of the firewater which Père Jules had once given me, but also to destroy the innards of the obstreperous doctor. I poured him a slug like Crippen pouring acid into the bath.

'Tanks.'

I didn't bother to correct his accent, leaving him to make a fool of himself.

'Tanks a million.' He poured himself another one. And with a wink, 'Nobiddy's perfit.'

Sadly, the caustic soda seemed to have little effect.

The Espace came up the drive. A pale and subservient version of her rebellious sister, Cécile looked understandably harassed. While her husband was cleaning his Porsche and rubbing cream into his hair, she had been picking up two of the children – Hortense from a riding lesson, Mathilde from music. The four girls were identically dressed: pleated skirt, ankle socks, blue cardigan and plaits. They looked as if they were on their way to an audition for *The Sound of Music*. Thierry lamented.

'Ballet, Ancient Greek, recorder. It never stops. They'll be the ruin of me.'

I would have loved to make Cécile laugh and do know a reasonably funny joke about a Scotsman, an Irishman and a very small nun, but Thierry had decided that it was time to leave.

'*En voiture!*' he commanded, then strode outside and began scolding his eldest daughter, who was in the process of loosening the wheel nuts of the Porsche – doubtless in order to kill her father.

'Leave Papa's toy alone, Aurore!'

Sheepishly she slipped the monkey-wrench back into the pocket of her cardy. We bowled down the drive to the disapproval of the Matou herd. The cattle-wagon followed behind, desperately trying to keep up. Thierry occasionally telephoned advice using his ultra-flat Nokia with its *Eine kleine Nachtmusik* ringtone.

'You not driving straight, woman. Keep to the right!'

The Plain of St Maure was like a miniature version of the Beauce. Huge skies crushed down upon a thin strip of brown land. Not a hedge for miles. Virtually treeless. Dilapidated corrugated iron barns, crooked telegraph poles, an apologetic copse, a weary cockerel, a distant tractor ploughing the thick clay, fallow fields, a flight of crows. . . . Welcome to desolation.

Thierry was over the moon. He'd found the bargain of the century. *Une perle*. The price? '*Quinze patates à peine*,' he told me proudly. What? He'd paid for the farm in potatoes? I was impressed by the tubercular economy of peasant France. Had he bought his car in carrots? Later, I found out that *une patate* in slang means a thousand quid in francs.

We arrived at the *lieu-dit* – the hamlet named Le Bosquet, a few kilometres north of Toison in the direction of Dolus. Everything was curiously singular. One farmhouse, one barn, one rotten roof, one hen, one puddle, one *château d'eau*. The French are specialists in water-towers, vast tall monstrosities looking like a concrete sculpture of an atomic cloud, invariably situated where they can be seen for miles.

'Know what this is? *Hein?*' He poked me.

Hell on earth?

'*Au-then-tique. Totalement au-then-tique.*'

He stormed into the farmhouse, pushing the double doors and causing the hinges to pop out of the crumbling wall. I protested. Surely he should knock.

'Knock? I own the place, *mon vieux. C'est moi le chef*. Bought the whole lot. *En viager*.'

Acheter en viager is a way of buying property cheap in France. You buy a house from its owner who has the right to remain in the property until he or she dies.

'When the old bird kicks the bucket . . . it's all mine!' He winked. 'We've put soap on the stone rim around the well.'

The he bawled: '*Aimée!?*' He took a pretty box with a pink ribbon from his briefcase. 'I've brought her some chocolates.'

I was surprised by his thoughtfulness. Maybe I'd got him wrong.

'She's diabetic!' he fell about laughing. I tried to edge him towards the well.

Dr Thierry strode around the one-room, soot-caked farmhouse breathing in the smell of old fat and cat's pee.

'*Beaucoup de cachet!* A lot of charm. *Les Angliches* are going to love it. They're buying anything and everything. Mind you, they're right. The French are too stupid. It's better to invest in real estate than in junk bonds. *Ça, c'est du solide!*'

He hit the wall and a large portion of plaster crumbled to the floor into a saucepan of elderly cabbage. Just then, Aimée, the owner, came in from the fields. She was ancient and healthy, with a ribbon in her hair, wearing a black flowery smock and brown wellies caked in authentic mud. She was as wiry and knotted as an olive tree.

The conversation which followed was in Thierry's version of peasant French.

'*Alors, la mère Nazelle. Ça va-t-y?*'

Which Thierry didn't speak and Aimée didn't understand. He tried again.

'*Ça va-t-y bien? Ça va-t-y mal?*'

Thierry put her lack of response down to her hearing.

'Deaf as a post, of course. But apart from that, as fit as a bloody fiddle. That's what comes from eating fresh vegetables all your life, the old cow. I'd better bring her some frozen hamburgers, *hein Aimée*?'

Aimée stared at him with a polite smile which expressed something in the region of, 'Piss off you urban Dracula.'

Cécile arrived at last, and was chastised for having lost her way. Yes, Thierry had the maps in his car, *mais quand même*. The picnic she had prepared in a pretty wicker basket included a homemade fruitcake which, according to Thierry, was not in the same league as the fruitcake his mother made.

'*En route!*' We hadn't even finished eating.

Then came the high spot of the afternoon. Walking back to the car, munching the remains of a piece of cake, Thierry suddenly slipped on a cowpat and fell flat on his back into a puddle of liquid shit. Suddenly Cécile and the girls burst out laughing. They laughed until they cried.

'*Vous trouvez ça drôle, vous?*' he steamed.

This was what they had been waiting for. Cécile looked twenty years younger and the kids looked like children again. I slipped Hortense five Euros and told her to tell Lou I'd pushed him.

On the way back to Allée Notre Dame Thierry put the Porsche heating on to dry out and the car stank like a blocked loo in a hammam. He authoritatively parked on arrival in the privet hedge and beckoned me across the road to view the parents' house.

'Look at that place. *Regarde-moi cette bicoque*. It's far too big. Far too expensive to run. Put them in a home and divide the place into flats. Make a fortune. A goldmine. Talk to Lou – she'll understand.'

He looked at me and winked. 'Nobiddy's parfect!'

For once I agreed with him.

12

I was invited to Christmas lunch *chez les Charpins*. This was to be my first opportunity to spend time with and, I hoped, to impress Lou's parents. But Christmas was not the best time to choose.

In ancient times, men lived in savage hordes. Deep down, the memory lingers on and families make the most of the annual gathering to dig up buried hatchets. On the surface everything seems to be goodwill and mistletoe, but underneath the marzipan lurks the Id. In the words of the eminent thinker Roland Barthes – one of whose books I had bought in order to impress the *agrégée* – come Christmas, we return to *le tuf archaïque* – the archaic bedrock.

The British make long-term preparations to ward off bloodshed. As early as November, supermarkets are raided as if the world was threatened with a stuffing shortage. The larder is packed with Paxo. Neighbours who don't move fast enough are silently derided. 'Poor fool. His turkey will be hollow.' The freezer is filled with exotic dishes no one wants – tempura of Pacific-caught scallops, deep-frozen Chinese noodles for sixteen. If the cousins from Yorkshire turn up unexpectedly, no problem – out with the winkles and the wok, and *à table*.

I had not left England unprepared. The Mazda hatchback was full of niceties, including one remarkable

Christmas pudding. It dated from 1998 and had once belonged to the opulent Emma Driver who had dumped me for an abject, cigar-smoking City trader. To avenge the insult, I nicked her pudding. It was lovingly stored in a tin portraying the Queen in uniform on horseback. At least one pleasure of which Emma Driver would be deprived. The trophy had since shrivelled and now looked like a camel's testicle.

I parked the Mazda with its bonnet in the privet hedge and took my festive plastic bag with the camel's undercarriage nestling next to the crackers. Strange as it may seem, there are no crackers in France. Or, to put it another way, there are, but they don't have them. I explained the party phenomenon to Lou. You each pull one end and it goes bang. Out pops a paper hat, a gadget – a plastic Horse Guard in nine pieces, or a mouse with a luminous nose – and a joke. Example:

- What a fog.
- I've seen worse.
- Where was that?
- Search me. Too foggy.

This joke has always made me fall about. However, once translated into Racinian French . . .

- *Mais quel brouillard épais!*
- *J'en ai vu de bien pire.*
- *Où est-ce que vous en avez vu de bien pire?*
- *J'en ai pas la moindre idée car, précisément, le brouillard était trop dense.*

. . . the joke seems somehow to lose its edge. Lou was doubtful as to the contribution my crackers were going to make to family jollity.

Over the wall, I could hear Lou's footsteps on the gravel. This was a crucial moment. I was tense. I kissed her on the cheek – a family greeting – and we walked up the small steps leading to the front door. From the kitchen, raised voices. Not another *clafoutis*?

Lou confirmed: '*Ça barde.*'

They were talking about Shakespeare? No. *Barder* turned out to mean to quarrel. There was a row in progress.

'*Il y a une couille dans le potage.*'

A testicle in the soup? Funny that. I've got another one in my bag.

The problem? Christmas lunch. Traditionally at Noël the Charpin family served turkey. Not this year. On his way back from Bulgaria by car, Laurent, President of the Loches branch of the Friends of Bulgaria Association, had stopped off in Bavaria where a friend had slipped him at a knockdown price a large amount of local venison which had fallen off the back of a lorry. Bringing the hoard home had been no easy business. The local butcher had dismantled the beast but the size of the animal was such that you couldn't get the bits into a freezer bag even with a shoe-horn and hammer. Every time he stopped to wet his whistle, Laurent had to get the game out of the boot and beg a place in the fridge.

And how did you cook the stuff once it was de-bagged? In the kitchen, dissension was rife. On our left the overnight marinators, on my right the cook-it-pink brotherhood. Rémi, the *gauchiste* SNCF train-driver brother, was of the opinion that game, the product of hunting, was unacceptably right-wing. At that point, Laurent, who had travelled hundreds of kilometres with his festering haunches, lost his cool.

'If that's the way you feel, you can all stuff it!! Eat Dylan's bloody canaries for all I care!'

Sylvie, depressed, drowned her sorrows in another bottle of rosé.

Festive hysteria set in. Henriette, Cécile's youngest, had been given a doll for Christmas. You spoke into a microphone concealed in its bodice and the message recorded was repeated out loud every time you pressed a button just above its plastic bum. Every twenty seconds or so, the house was filled with a loud, tinny voice screaming, 'Bugger off!' Thierry, furious, was heading an enquiry to discover the culprit, '*Quelle petite salope a enregistré cette saloperie?*' Mathilde's present was a bunny called Vanessa (after Vanessa Paradis) who spent her time quivering and shitting in her cage. Emmeline had lost her dentures down the *sofa*. Dylan, his left leg nervously jumping up and down like a pneumatic drill, was staring into mid-distance, listening to rap on his Walkman. His large cellophane-wrapped coffee-table book on Flemish Art lay unopened under the tree. Edouard had learned the ingredients of the Christmas pudding off by heart and walked around the house reciting them to himself: raisins, sultanas, nuts, eggs, cream, owl's snot, brandy. Gisèle was frenetically screwing and unscrewing the 270 light bulbs which decorated the tree and which stubbornly refused to flash. She was very excited. She whispered her secret in my ear. Going through Laurent's drawers she had come across her present – a heart-shaped red satin G-string adorned with black fluffy pompoms –

tucked away behind his socks. He'd obviously bought it for her and hidden it. *Le petit coquin!* The naughty boy! In the meantime Laurent was desperately trying to phone somewhere outside the reach of his mobile, while Cécile lovingly ironed Thierry's famous red jacket.

'Christmas wouldn't be Christmas without Thierry's famous red jacket!!'

Lou had decided to compose a *chemin de table* – a leafy decoration to run along the white linen tablecloth. She ripped the ivy from the ivy-clad – and what rapidly proved to be the ivy-supported – garden wall, which subsequently collapsed. Vanessa set about eating the ivy, which induced instant diarrhoea. Ernesto, believing that the rabbit, like a snail, was emptying itself to become comestible, slavered in anticipation. Mathilde decided to kill Ernesto with an electric carving knife – fortunately supplied without batteries. Sylvie, pissed, distributed silver aluminium freezer trays which, once bent, were perfect for wrapping up small presents like Korean soles, and endeavoured to get the family to coalesce to take a group photograph with her new camera which she was holding backwards.

Monsieur et Madame Charpin, Lou's parents, seemed a shade bewildered by the turn events had taken. Lou's mother was a gracious, delicate lady in an elegant blue dress. She had the same laconic smile as Lou but was less conflictual by nature, slipping away in times of stress for a *mise en plis*. These hair-dos were purely strategic and her only way of finding a bit of peace. She'd already had two since Tuesday. Monsieur Charpin was round, smiling and not quite as tall as his wife. They were both extremely polite to me. I even sensed a kind of compassion. They had doubtless

witnessed an endless string of suitors and couldn't tell
one from the other.

Monsieur Charpin was a retired vet. It was not
uncommon in the vicinity of the house to stumble upon
a dog with a limp or a hedgehog with a cold hoping that
the magician would slip out and give them a fix. His
other passion was for local goat cheese. Religiously I lis-
tened to him explain the Four Seasons of the St Maure.
The spring version was the unsalted, freshly curdled
variety which was shedding its whey like a perspiring
nymphette on a tennis court. Delicious with chives
and new garlic – the cheese, that is, not the nymphette.
The summer cheese was the freshly salted kind, soft,
delicate, simple, sunny – a perfect cheese for the beach.
In its mellow incarnation, the St Maure moves into its
autumnal phase, more resistant, dense, pithy, perfect
with a deep amber Vouvray. A cheese for a hammock
on a long September dusk. But Monsieur Charpin's
favourite, his secret passion, was the winter St Maure, a
cheese matured for months, hard, brittle, mature, rich,
as fragile as porcelain, *la quintessence du chèvre*.

He had his own special method of *affinage* – the
method of coaxing cheeses to maturity. They were kept
on the top of an Henri II-style *buffet* in the kitchen.
Every day he would take a chair, climb on it and, with
fervour, give his herd of beloved cheeses a delicate half-
turn – like a *remueur* with bottles of champagne.
Desperate to win his approval, I climbed on a chair
to observe the process wearing a paper hat from the
crackers. Lou passed through the kitchen.

'*Tu as l'air con avec ton chapeau.*'

Bon.

When her mobile rang, I was immediately taken
with a cosmic foreboding. I *knew* it was that bastard

Gérard. On Christmas Day I had been hoping to have Mademoiselle Charpin to myself. *Merde!* My neck muscles stiffened. Lou seemed perturbed. Had tragedy struck? Had another toy poodle pissed on his wheels?

'*Je vois.* Of course. *Je comprends. J'arrive.*'

J'arrive? What the hell was she talking about?

'*Pauvre Gérard,*' she sighed.

Pauvre, mon cul.

'He's got a problem.'

Tremendous.

'I'm going to have to go.'

I was firm. 'Then I'm coming with you.'

'Why?'

'Because I'm good at problems.'

I had no idea what the problem was, but there was no question of Lou providing a solution alone. We gave the venison a hug and jumped into the car. I extracted the toolbox from under the seat.

'What are you doing?'

'Preparing to fix it.'

'Fix the goose?'

'He's broken his *goose?*'

The tragedy was quick to emerge. Gérard was having Christmas lunch with *maman.* The maid had left to see her family in Portugal and there was no one to carve. What a pickle. Not that I quite understood Lou's concern. If you're stinking rich, all you have to do is to phone Inter-Goose. They'd send a technician within the hour who'd bone the bugger in a trice.

But no. All this, of course, was Gérard's skulduggery. He just wanted an excuse to see his Loulou, I said accusingly. Not at all, she assured me. This was not like him. It was just another sign of the deep depression looming off his coastline.

'What a coincidence,' I lied. 'I'm an ace with geese.' The only thing I'd ever carved in my life was a boned breast of turkey at a Cubs' bonfire when I was seven, but I wasn't letting on.

'I'm surprised,' I added with mock disbelief, 'that he doesn't know how to carve.' This sentence involved a subjunctive *qu'il ne sache pas découper* of which I was not displeased. 'In England', I continued, 'gentlemen know how to handle poultry.'

The Mazda arrived at Boulevard Béranger in front of the Mortier palace. I was about to ring the bell when Lou took a key out of her bag. *Allons donc!* She must be on poultry patrol more often than I would like to think. We walked across the gravel of the courtyard which crunched like Rice Crispies underfoot. The large white stone house was richly decorated and sinister, like a Christmas morgue. Flashing lights did their best to liven it all up. In vain. On each side of the entrance bay trees stood at attention. In the vestibule hung lush tapestries, one of a medieval damsel being nuzzled by a very forward unicorn. On another, an army of bloodthirsty warriors attacked each other with kebabs. Around the base of a huge Christmas tree a pile of mock presents in silver paper to give the impression that the occupants were liked and loved.

Gérard wore a hangdog look on his face. I told him the fog joke to cheer him up but he didn't listen. We crossed a series of reception rooms each as charmless as the next. On the wall of the kitchen was ranged a vast collection of copper saucepans, next to a giant professional la Cornue stove – a little excessive for cooking poached eggs on toast.

We extracted the goose from the oven with some difficulty, it weighed about nineteen kilos. Lou stuck

a knife in its thigh. It didn't squeal, which was a
good sign. The juice was, however, still pink. It would
need at least another forty-five minutes. I stuck an
Elastoplast over the wound and shoved it back in.
Gérard left to inform his mother.

I decided to prepare myself for the operation.
Carving requires accuracy and relaxation. An indoor
pool in what had once had been the stables had caught
my eye as we crossed the courtyard. Lou remained
in one of the salons reading a huge coffee-table book
on something essential like extinct parrots.

I walked back across *crunch-crunch* the breakfast-
food courtyard. Two large glass doors slid silently
back, opening on to the Turkish-bath warmth inside.
I didn't have any trunks with me – they are not an
essential part of the goose-carver's equipment – but, in
an insolent mood, decided bathing in the nude was
what was called for. I dived straight in and splashed
around like a happy whale singing, 'A life on the ocean
wave' as the winter cold shone in frosty flowers against
the glass of the partition doors. This was the life. I was
made for luxury. This was the way to spend Christmas,
wallowing in *Le Grand Bleu*. The pursuit of Miss
Charpin, hazardous and gruelling as it might be, did
also have its captivating moments.

When I re-entered Château Gloom, Gérard was
quick to notice my wet hair. He went even paler. A new
cloud crossed his face. Had I dared take a dip without
the permission of the lifeguard?

'I trust you blew your nose?'

What the hell was he talking about? We strode once
again back across the courtyard to the pool.

'Look.'

We examined the surface of the pool.

'What's that?'

The surface of the pool, which was in the process of regaining a semblance of calm after the passage of the human dolphin, was scattered with tiny translucent jellyfish.

'Tadpoles?'

Gérard was furious. 'Snot.'

'I beg your pardon?'

'*De la morve.* You didn't blow your nose before swimming.' He handed me a shrimping net. 'My mother must never see this. Fish them out.'

'Them?'

'The snots.' He stormed back to the house.

Madame Mortier came down. She must have been about 150. Dressed from head to toe in black, deathly white and heavily made up, she looked like a crow dressed for the carnival in Rio. I passed her a cracker to cheer her up. 'It's a game!' I shouted. 'You pull at each end and it goes bang.' We pulled. It banged. She didn't even jump. Her fuses must have blown long ago. The joke fell to the ground. I picked it up.

'I say I say I say.'

She looked at me as if I was insane.

'What is yellow and goes around at 33 revolutions per minute?'

Silence.

'Answer: a long-playing omelette.'

Silence. From her dead branch, the crow eyed me with scorn. Then: 'In France, monsieur, we do not listen to omelettes.'

All this was beyond her ken. Her son was rolling in it. He ran a flourishing business. What the hell was Lou Charpin doing with a prankster who listened to eggs?

The kitchen was issuing smoke signals. I slipped into

an apron, doffed some protective gloves while Lou laid the table. I transferred the goose from the tray to a carving dish by shoving a long wooden spoon up what I presumed was its backside. The bird was oddly constructed. Where did it start and where did it stop? It had very long arms – if birds have arms – and a great deal of elbow. I turned it over and pushed the knife into its breast. *Ddooiingngg*. The thing was all bone. If you gave it a knock with a spoon it echoed. Just like Gérard's mum.

I found this all surprising. Poultry should nowadays be sold with dotted lines along which to cut. I had a look on the shelves for a Goose book and found a plan of the beast in a priceless nineteenth-century copy of the *Larousse de la Cuisine* which I unfortunately had to consult with my fatty fingers. With the help of the diagram I made an incision. *Splurge*. Stuffing spurted out and on to the floor – apricots, prunes, couscous, old wellies, snot from the pool. I picked it all up with a deft finger, pushed it back in and closed the hole with a another bit of Elastoplast. The goose began to look like a bruiser after fifteen rounds with Mike Tyson.

Euréka. In the drawer of the kitchen table, an electric carving-knife. Just what the doctor ordered. ZZZZZZ. Fantastic. The knife was devastatingly efficient. In a trice I cut the whole thing into two. It fell apart. So did I. Fun at last. I then cut each half into two again. I now had four quarters of a one-time goose lolling on the plate in front of me. It all looked a shade 'destroy', but the great advantage of the quartering process was that if they didn't like it they could easily stick the thing back together with Superglue. At the back of the fridge loitered a tired lettuce. I cut the lettuce into shreds – ZZZZZZ – and threw the remnants over the goose quarters for decoration. Classy. I then poured the fat from the bottom of the dish all over the meat. Goose fat is very good for the arteries. In South-West France, where they brush their teeth with *foie gras*, heart disease is unheard of.

I then served at table. Madame Mortier and her offspring looked a little taken aback. This was not how the *bonne* did it.

'Goose', I announced. *À L'Anglaise!*

'*Ah bon.*'

'The traditional method. Cut into four. Queen Victoria's favourite. Wouldn't touch a goose carved any other way.'

They were sufficiently snobbish to swallow anything. Including the goose. We left them at table eyeing their large portions of mutilated poultry.

'And should you have any difficulty with the dessert,' I said airily, '*pas de problème*. Just give us a call.'

Back at l'Allée Notre Dame, chaos reigned. You could feel the tension over the wall. Such was the urgency that we left the Mazda in the safe hands of the nuns who, heedful of the tragedy unfolding around the Christmas table, had decided to run a valet service.

Inside the house, tribal divisions were rife. One half of the family had eaten the venison pink and it tasted like rubber blubber. The other half were still waiting for theirs to cook. Sylvie, in a desperate attempt to heal the wounds, had persuaded the marinators to eat the meal backwards so that the whole family could at last congregate around the table. They had thus started with the pudding. I had forgotten to tell them to cook it. Result, instead of steaming it for four hours in a bain-marie they had eaten the camel's testicle raw and were on the point of calling a doctor. Thierry and Cécile's offspring were screaming with angst. They had exhausted their batteries and their dollies could no longer say 'Bugger off.' Ernesto, in a fit of frustration, had eaten the rabbit's cage. Emmeline had lost a letter from her brand new ivory Scrabble and was dismantling the sofa. Gisèle had opened her present which turned out to be a bracelet. Why a bracelet? She was at a loss. Where were the knickers?

In order to escape the shrapnel, I went out into the garden and bumped into Laurent who was having a secret and passionate conversation on his mobile in what I presumed to be pidgin Bulgarian. He looked embarrassed at having been caught red-handed.

'Don't tell me. You speak Bulgarian.'

'No, honestly, Laurent.'

'Don't tell me . . .'

At that moment, Gisèle emerged from the house, a collapsed Dylan in her arms. Their son had acute conjunctivitis. Look at his eyes. They were all red. Poor little lamb, it must be the pollen. Laurent went out of his mind.

'Pollen! That's not pollen. Whoever heard of pollen in December? He's stoned.'

'Stoned?'

'*Il est complètement foncedé, ton fils.*'

Two linguistic remarks are needed here. One *verlan*. *Défoncé* backwards gives *foncedé*. Stoned. Two, the use of the possessive article. In French, when you want to get rid of a problem, you attribute it to someone else. Our son – *notre fils* – instantly became *ton fils*.

'How did he do that?'

'What anyone does to get stoned, *ma chérie. Il a fumé du shit.*'

Gisèle's world collapsed. For her, Dylan was still nine and tucked up in bed reading *Bambi*. He couldn't be stoned! She started to faint. I had to support her which was no mean feat as she was already supporting Dylan.

At that point, Rémi came out into the garden, looking sombre. He took me off to a dark corner, his sinister, menacing look mitigated by the Christmas pullover of two frolicking elks which Sylvie had knitted for him. We stopped under a dripping fir tree.

'*Tu fricotes avec ma petite soeur,*' he snarled.

I wasn't quite sure what *fricoter* meant but I got the gist.

'*Attention. Fais attention.*'

He raised a warning finger. Any jiggery pokery and the family mafia hit squad would be out for my blood. Then the hoodlum lurched off into the darkness of the *potager*.

I was stunned. The day was falling apart. Dylan was an addict, Emmeline had gone berserk, Edouard was reciting the Christmas pudding, Laurent was spooning in Bulgarian and I had just received a death threat from the SNCF.

Suddenly, there was the noise of a shelf collapsing in the potting shed. Silence. Then Sylvie's voice rang out over the winter garden, shrill and tipsy, singing a forlorn *a capella* version of 'Some Day My Prince Will Come'.

You can't beat Christmas.

13

On Boxing Day I invited Lou to dinner.

The railwayman's magazine *La Vie du Rail* recently featured aphrodisiacal food. It recommended oysters, which tickle the palate and other less accessible regions. I bought a dozen to experiment. Sadly fruitless; impossible to open them. I tried the works – screwdriver, hammer, jemmy – but no go. I threw them at the wall but only managed to damage the plaster. A most unimpressionable mollusc.

In the last resort I swapped the erotic for the exotic. *Un crapaud dans le trou* would do the trick. Nothing more delicious than toad-in-the-hole. I spent a happy afternoon rolling my rissoles of minced pork and herbs on my thighs like Carmen in a cigar factory.

But all was not well. The gurgling radiators woke me up in the middle of the night with their rendition of Handel's *Water Music*, and the next day I was tense. Lou also looked on edge. Her anxiety was imprinted on her forehead, the frown taking the form of a seagull poised for flight.

'What are you doing for the New Year, Mike?'

The pronoun took me by surprise. 'You', not 'we'? In my unconscious I had presumed that 'we' would be somewhere surrounded by streamers, warm champagne, Canadian lobsters and goodwill. True, in France, the decision as to where you are going for the New Year and who you are going with tends to be taken in the preceding January.

'I thought . . . probably yes . . . that we would, you know . . .' I blustered.

'*Ça ne va pas être possible, Mike.*'

The seagull frown took off landed on my forehead.

'Before we met, I'd promised Gérard . . .'

Encore lui! The painful truth emerged. Lou was the model for the new Mortier Optical catalogue. They'd already done the castles, the vineyards, the hunt – now they were going to shoot the final sequences for the new tinted polarising sunglasses – where? In Bognor? No, sir. On Mauritius. Lou was contrite but she couldn't let Gérard down on page 34, could she? There was, of course, absolutely no reason to be angry or jealous.

Far be it from me to suspect a jilted, bitter, depressed, designing provincial optician. I endeavoured to be elegant by flashing a few subjunctives around – the *Je ne sais pas que tu aies rien à me reprocher* kind of job – but my beloved wasn't listening. Her mind was already on the beach.

She did try to cheer me up, however, by teaching me a new word. We had a game. Every day, a useless word. Today it was *splanchnique*. Meaning appertaining to the visceral. My rissoles tasted *splachnique*. But today my heart was not in it. Too bad. Don't worry about me, I thought self-pityingly. I'll just sit alone in the rain munching a *biscotte*.

During the night, the radiators gurgled in compassion. The next morning, at least the birds were happy with the leftovers of my toad-in-the-hole.

Quelle vie.

*

Et voilà. She'd gone. Left. Done a bunk. *Partie.*
Évanouie. Elle a pris la poudre d'escampette. Stupid
bloody expression.

Until the very last moment I'd hoped. That the
taxi wouldn't come. That there would be a strike. This
was France, after all. Just a tiny protest movement. An
air-traffic controller who tripped on the rug. A baggage-
handler who'd caught his finger in a swing door. But
no. For once nothing.

At 7.20 a.m. off she went. *Ni vu ni connu,* as they
say. I remained alone in her flat. Alone with her clothes,
her perfume hanging in the air, her packet of Kleenex.
Sniff sniff. I dried my eyes. She'd not even forgotten
her passport. Mortier had won. You have conquered,
oh optical Frog. I'd been dumped. Stranded. *Ariadne
auf Lilo.* The pair of them had left for the Indian
Ocean, leaving me stranded in the doldrums.

I found an atlas and drew a red ring around
Mauritius. I evoked the hotel, with its jerry-built shacks
on stilts and its rat-infested, bird-flu-redolent thatched
roofs. What a dump. After ten hours of cramped
torture cooped on a plane, they'd sit down to frozen
shrimps served by underpaid slaves in a colonial dining
room. Gérard would float around the pool on his inflatable Quad, the sod. With my long-distance cyber
remote control I teleguided piranhas under his pédalo.
Bonnes vacances, Gérard.

And what, I asked myself, were the sleeping arrangements to be, *hein*? *Chambre à part,* Lou had assured me.
Each in his own room. You couldn't fool me. I could
see him on all fours crawling along the corridor in the
middle of the night, pleading, inveigling, scratching at
her door. *Let me in. I've got problems with my goose.*

Tours went sad. The once animated rue de Bordeaux

had lost its edge. On the majestic town square, the fountains had brewer's droop. The plane trees along the Boulevard Béranger peeled with the cold. Between me and the town the current no longer flowed. The stuffed elephant, Fritz, in the gardens of the museum lno longer looked in danger of running rampant as he had some hundred years ago. Lou had left and thrown the switch. It had all gone out. I decided to retreat to Toison.

The village, I discovered, had been invaded by an army of Father Christmases. Like Arsène Lupin, they were climbing walls, holding on to chimneystacks, shinning up drainpipes. One poor devil was hanging from the guttering, throttled by his gift wrapping. The wind had blown another one right off the roof and he was lying face down in the middle of the road like a drunk on 14 July. La Veuve Cognette, who used to run the Toison d'Or, had decorated her barn door with empty gift-wrapped boxes which banged and rattled in the cold wind.

Mouzay was even worse. Marcellin was glum again. Monique had left to rejoin her husband Louis on his North Sea oil-rig. True to form, he had wanted to follow her and had asked me along. But the idea of spending New Year's Eve cooped up with Marcellin and a box of streamers in a Citroën Picasso parked facing the North Sea was not my idea of a party.

The invitation was not as generous as it sounds. Marcellin needed a driver. The Tasmalou had decided, in a fit of high spirits, to decorate the murky windows of the Toison d'Or, covered in a thick coat of tar, the result of fifty years of non-stop Gauloises. To this end they purchased several spray cans of instant snow at Bricorama. When they had finished the café, they went

on to decorate the windows of Marcellin's Picasso, in
order to cheer the poor devil up. The effect was artistic
but dangerous. It was like driving a sleigh towards the
North Pole. Even the scraper couldn't get the stuff off.
It was Père Jules who came up with the solution. All
they had to do was pour a bottle of *gnôle* into the windscreen squirters. *Eureka*. Snow and wipers melted in
a trice. Unfortunately, Marcellin was stopped by the
gendarmerie for a routine check and was pronounced
drunk on the fumes. He lost his licence for three months
and was deprived of his North Sea jaunt.

I would, however, drive him to Loches to pick up
Monique's Christmas present. The Garage du Mail was
a collection point for the mail order firm La Redoute.
With a slight blush Marcellin showed me the page in
the catalogue: a pink satin slip and thong combo. The
slip, 90 per cent polyamide, was finished in white lace,
with a saucy slit revealing the left thigh. Adjustable
spaghetti straps and pink bows between the cups.
Perfect for driving the school bus.

Coming out of the Garage, I bumped into Ariane
Tricot. Her lips burst into a fiery, pyrotechnical smile.

'Je suis super contente de vous voir, Maï-quel.'

Tremendous.

'Alors, la petite prof?' She was trying to do her down.
'Comment va-t-elle? Vous fêtez où le Nouvel An?'
Ariane obviously thought we'd be off to Butlins.

'Nous partons à Marrakech,' I lied.

Fool that I was. The Tricots were leaving for
Marrakech as well. In fact, *le tout Loches* was heading
soukwards. We must, we simply *must*, get together. I
lied again. No, we were in fact leaving for the Sahara
for a remote oasis famous for being untraceable on
any map.

Ariane was disappointed, but intrigued by my mail-order parcel. '*On lui achète des cadeaux à La Redoute?*' she asked nosily.

Yes. A bus-driver's outfit. I promised Ariane that we would meet up on our return.

'*Au revoir, Ariane!*'

'*Au revoir, Maï-quel.*'.

Her *Maï-quel*, once devastating, left me cold. My heart was in the Indian Ocean.

Alone in the house, I sat down for a few hours and wrote the following text in French:

La maison, au lever du soleil, est un rêve automnal. Embrumée de volutes nébuleuses, esquissée dans des pastels à la Chardin, la demeure, cachottière, entre et sort de l'épaisseur d'un rêve. Un soleil orange, lourd et lointain, se hisse au-dessus de la frontière estompée du jour. C'est l'hiver, saison où tout, herbe, branche, racine, écorce, s'imprègne de la feuille morte.

Translation:

The house, at dawn, was an autumnal dream. Enveloped by curlicues of mist, sketched, in Chardin-like dull pastels, the house played hide and seek with the eye. Now you see me, now you don't. The heavy orange disk of the distant morning sun opened its slumbent eye over the blurred line of the horizon. Winter infused all, grass, trees, roots, bark, with the pungent perfume of dead leaves.

In short, a load of crap.

Why bother to impress an *agrégée* with my flashy French, while she was at that precise moment fending off goose-hunters in the corridors of her tropical-fun palace?

The next day it was all too much. I couldn't start the year without Lou Charpin. We had to be close. Distance was unacceptable. I returned to the Allée Notre Dame. Cars were parked any old how. The apoplectic gentleman from over the road had gone vermilion. They should all have come out of the houses on the stroke of midnight and parked on the other side of the road. They hadn't. Western civilization was doomed.

I caressed the old cracked wall with its decorative lace of ivy and its wonky brickwork. I loved this wall. It was Lou's wall. On the other side, deep in the entrails of the kitchen, the family Charpin were no doubt at this very moment tearing each other to shreds. Without me. I was Pyramus in *A Midsummer Night's Dream*.

'O *wall! O sweet, o lovely wall!*'

I was the forlorn lover at the end of *In the Mood for Love*, whispering his passion into the old disjointed stones.

The proximity of the family was not enough. I wanted to be even closer. If I couldn't be with Lou, then I would eat her.

I drove like a bat out of hell to Vouvray. Miracle! On New Year's morning the charcuterie Hardouin was open. That's what I call service! You never know when some lovelorn fool is going to need a last-minute *andouillette*.

Back at the house, I ceremoniously unpacked the feast. It took me an hour to coax the fire to produce the glowing embers I needed. I cleaned the mushrooms, chopped the garlic and parsley, sautéed a few taut little charlotte potatoes and opened a bottle of 1995 mellow Vouvray, rich, tart, honeyed – divine after twenty-three minutes in the fridge.

À table. I then placed the golden, crisp, butter-soaked soft-centred potatoes on a large cracked oval serving dish. In the middle of the plate lay the *andouillette*, hot from the wood fire, its skin seared, torn, with its pungent smell of smoky innards, and finally the *girolles*, redolent with their tang of oak leaves, set off by the last-minute toss in *une noce de beurre* with parsley and garlic.

'*À toi, Lou,*' I toasted her. *Absente de mon lit, présente à ma table.*

A second bottle of the ever-amber Vouvray opened itself as if by a miracle. Happily pissed, I sat on the bench in what had become a pleasantly warm, glowing garden and, facing the evening sky, sang my favourite song southwards. '*Ma Préférence*' by Julien Clerc: *Mais elle est/ma préférence à moi.*

With unfound delicacy, the dogs of the Matou chorus joined in and echoed my feelings from the neighbouring farmyard.

Ma préférence à moi.

14

Was I paranoid? Could Lou Charpin be using me?

She returned from Mauritius sounding like Ariane 'en super forme', totally impervious to my comments on the monotony of shellfish and the incidence of supine opticians in the corridors of luxury hotels. I was showered with presents: a seashell necklace which made me look like a bank clerk arriving in Honolulu, a T-shirt for a pygmy on which was inscribed *Kiss Me Quick* in dialect, and – the gift I treasured most – a tin box containing some fresh vanilla pods. The pods cheered me up a lot. A pod was personal, different, meaningful. I didn't know quite what to do with them and slipped a handful into my boxer-shorts drawer, to lend them an exotic perfume. We then left to see a film by the ex-hero of the New Wave, Jacques Rivette.

In the course of the projection I became aware of the fact that I was sitting on a rather sticky pod. Moving it to a more comfortable position by means of tactical contractions of the bum muscles provided an excellent remedy against any boredom induced by the Nouvelle Vague.

Lou's skin, bronzed by hours of idling on beaches, did not bear the mark of sunglasses. Did Gérard just take a few snaps before inviting his model to join him in a more pleasurable leisure activity? I casually made the remark. She replied that I would do well to curb all sardonic comments about grass huts, lobsters and bi-focals.

January is the month of New Year presents – *les étrennes*. Visits are made to members of the family who have not been seen since the same period the preceding year and who, had it not been for *les étrennes*, would never be seen again. Bernard and Denise, Lou's aunt and uncle, were a prime example. They ran a small chain of DIY supermarkets which opened late at night to cater for obsessives who couldn't get to sleep before they had fixed the tap.

Denise, small, plump and welcoming, opened the door. In her flowery dress with its lacy trimmings she looked like a Laura Ashley hot-water bottle.

'*Tiens! Les jeunes!*'

Which I took to be a compliment.

'*Vous êtes donc le fameux Mikaël.*'

The adjective *fameux* must mean that I had been spoken about and was a new commodity.

'*Le copain anglais de notre chère Loulou.*'

Copain implied that we'd been friends since the Pony Club at the age of five and excluded all passion and intensity. *Amant* or lover would have been more my cup of tea, but this was a lot to expect from a hot-water bottle.

Bernard was a leading light in the local Rotary Club and extremely proud of his region. There were water-colours of the Loire Valley on the wall, embroidered cushions of the châteaux on the armchairs, and obscure local proverbs, of the 'an early worm heralds no good' variety on the decorative plates. The table was groaning under the weight of local goodies – *rillons*, *rillettes*, head, ears, tails, trotters, eyebrows, undercarriage. A pig in kit form.

Bernard bemoaned the state of France. What the country lacked was a politician of the ilk of *la dame de fer* – our own blue-rinsed, iron-willed Mrs T. Someone to lick it into shape. It had missed the boat and was rapidly sinking into decline. Too many *fonctionnaires*, too many *bolcheviques*. To cheer him up I offered him a chunk of pork. Denise looked at me in horror.

'*C'est interdit!*'

Forbidden? Bernard seemed an unlikely convert to Islam. Hadn't Lou spoken of his problem? Denise asked. I awaited the explanation with bated breath.

'*La constipation, évidemment!*' She passed me the plate. 'Do have some brawn, Mikaël.'

The rigours of constipation could, Bernard explained, as the *charcuterie* did its rounds, be abated thanks to existing palliatives – osmotic laxatives, lubrifying laxatives, and, of course, our old friends the rectal laxatives.

'Do have some more *pâté*.'

The market was rich in expedients, he went on. There was Spagulax, for instance, whose husk increased the weight of the faeces and modified their consistency.

'A sliver of *andouilllette*?'

And Parlax – which, however, over-generous in paraffin, could lead to excessive anal secretion.

'I do hope you don't find the *rillettes* too greasy?'

'Not at all. *Pas du tout.*'

Sadly, none of these miracle cures could do anything to cure the condition. The block was rock hard. Bernard banged on the table. This was no run-of-the-mill constipation. This was mahogany constipation. They were at a loss as to what to do. I was on the point of suggesting a Black & Decker drill from the shop downstairs or a bottle of Père Jules's snow-melting *gnôle*, when Lou,

in an attempt to ingratiate me with her family, asked
the question.

'And what of British constipation, Mikaël? Do tell.'

Taken aback, I nevertheless manage to wax lyrical
as to the relative simplicity of the English digestive
system compared with its French counterpart. On the
one hand, a Congregationalist chapel, empty, echoing
and totally devoid of ornament and interest, on the
other side, a baroque cathedral, full of statuary and
artwork, niches, and apses inspiring awe and worship.
Rather elegant, but no one was listening.

Bernard's second passion was painting. The attractive
watercolour Touraine landscapes on the walls turned
out to be the work of the master plumber himself.
I started to examine them when Bernard intervened,
cutting short any desire to compliment.

'They lack flow,' he said dismissively. 'Like wine,
they're corked. Look closely, Monsieur Sadler, at *Le
Verger de Monts*.'

I peered obligingly into the aforesaid orchard.
Examined close up, the grapes did, it was true, look
like dried rabbits' turds. Denise had apparently wanted
him to paint her in the nude, but it was not to be.
Bernard's condition precluded sensuality. He recited
a pastiche of a famous Alexandrine from *Le Cid* by
Corneille to capture his personal tragedy:

'*O blocage! O bouchon! Occlusion intestine!*'

Hoping to change the subject, I offered Denise a
chocolate. A terrible mistake. It was Bernard's turn
to look askance.

'But . . . Monsieur Sadler! Surely you have heard of
Denise's tube!'

Bernard took a piece of paper and a pencil. An explanation was necessary. There exists, at the bottom of

the French digestive tube, at the point at which the estuary flows into the ocean, a siphon which prevents the downflow from ebbing back up. Denise's problem was her siphon.

'*Je suis un martyr du clapet, Monsieur Sadler.*'

At that precise moment the phone rang, and Lou used the ensuing conversation with a supplier of hydrochloric acid – another radical solution for constipation? – as an excuse to leave. On the landing, she was profuse in her thanks. It was really *sympa* of me to escort her to her aunt and uncle, she said. *Sympa*? Is that what I was reduced to? The *copain sympa*? When she spent the rest of her time wearing Polaroids in the tropics?

I was assailed by a terrible doubt. Was I merely a pleasant stop-gap?

Fernande was Monsieur Charpin's sister. She shared her brother's love of animals and lived alone in a pretty cottage in the village of Boussay, surrounded by twenty stray cats, two parrots who hated each other's guts, and an army of gerbils. A concrete menagerie decorated the overgrown garden. She wore a large pair of tortoise-shell Buddy Holly glasses and drove an authentic mini-Cooper from the 1960s, with an elegant pair of leather driving gloves and, when the window was down, a linen Fangio-style helmet.

Lou introduced me and immediately disappeared. It didn't take me long to figure out why.

'Oh yes, of course, I see so it's you, Lou's boyfriend I trust you don't think I'm too forward I've heard so much about you you being different well if not different let's say English shall we which is different enough although I've always had a bit of a weakness for the English I've even got a tin box and on the tin box is a decoration of a typically English village with thatched roofs, snow everywhere, the village pond frozen over, the snowman with his carrot and children on their sledge let's face it a bit *cucul* a bit of a pain really but nonetheless *cucul* or not it's in that tin that I keep my tea just like my sister so every time I open the box I think of my sister in St Radégonde who is either having one of her endless *mise en plis* or having a cup of tea herself but please excuse me I believe you wanted to say something . . .?'

'Actually, Fernande, yes I—'

'How funny I mean what a coincidence your way of pronouncing my name Fernande in Boussay I have let's call it a little circle of friends not a salon no no that would be far too grand just a little circle it's true people say to me don't you get bored out of your tiny mind Fernande heavens no because every week we have for instance lunch or in my case tea because since my hip I'm not too hot on standing up for hours over a *ragoût* in the kitchen so I'm more often than not the tea lady which I keep in my box with the English village but you know all about that steady as you go Fernande and in my circle I have a favourite I know I shouldn't have a favourite but Marcelle is so elegant every week a different hat which always goes so well with her *tailleur* not like me of course a craggy old bohemian surrounded by cats and Marcelle and I we love to watch a television programme which unlike most television programmes makes you think *ça travaille la ciboule* if you see what I mean unlike most television programmes and so we watch *Questions pour un champion* together and the other day there was a question about sport now I don't actually follow sport this question was about football would you believe and I knew the answer the answer was Lizarazu now Lizarazu doubtless doesn't mean anything to you he's Basque you see from the Basque country not one of those nasty Basques with a balaclava and a Tommy gun no a very pleasant Basque who plays for *Les Bleus* that's what we call out national football team *Allez les Bleus* and Marcelle was so impressed by my sporting knowledge which was as I have I believe intimated a pure fluke God knows how I know anything about dribbling Basques I of course mean dribbling in the football sense i.e. running with the ball at your feet not dribbling slavering far be it from me to intimate that Basques slaver nonetheless Marcelle impressed by my answer said *'Chapeau Fernande'* *chapeau* being what you say in French as if you were taking off your hat to someone as an expression of admiration *'Chapeau Fernande'* which brings me back to what I was saying because Marcelle says Fernande in exactly the same way as you . . .'

Fernande was sitting pert and upright on the sofa in front of me, as fresh and bubbling as a *flûte de champagne*. While she spoke you could do a good number of things: knit a pullover, pick your nose, throw peanuts into the fish tank, dream of *la croupe* of Lou Charpin, compose Chapter One of your sensitive first novel, throttle the spaniel, slowly move a vanilla pod from one side of your bum to the other. What you couldn't do was to interrupt Fernande.

'. . . of course I know you're dying to ask the question everyone asks me no one can understand how I can face living in Boussay day in day out yes I can see the question perched on the edge of your lips, I can see it like a butterfly perched to fly I know yes I am sometimes a shade fanciful but although I shouldn't let on yes as a young girl I did actually put pen to paper and compose a few poems I know you're dying to say Fernande you must be bored arseless now don't think being bored arseless is an expression I use every day I picked it up from my nephew Dylan who has at least the grace if that's the word to be honest and the last time he came here intimated to his mother Gisèle that he was bored arseless and to be honest I don't blame him because Gisele was it must be said in the process of boring me arseless as well although Emmeline refused to let me use the word in Scrabble the other day arseless counts three I said no go she replied although you ought to know what you're talking about Boussay being the first place in the world one might want to go if one was seeking to be bored in the aforesaid fashion but of course she's wrong you only have to do like me and hide behind the lace curtains . . .'

At that precise moment I had three cats on my knees, a budgerigar on my head and a gerbil in each ear.

'. . . and you just watch them troop by Mademoiselle Sicard she's eighty-four and still a virgin left it a bit late to make up for lost time I have a bit of a giggle to myself you old faggot I whisper behind the curtain which muffles everything I say thank God because if she ever knew what I whispered into my lace curtain I couldn't even go out of the front door but it's good to get it all out of your system I haven't got a psy as they say nowadays I have no desire to stretch out on a sofa and talk about myself in front of a total stranger and of course I don't smoke dope although Dylan did offer to supply me with a *pétard* as he put it if ever the urge took me no I just hide behind my lace curtains and let it all hang out on Sunday mornings when all the do-gooders troop off to Mass and Colin the priest arrives late and has trouble extracting his stomach from his *deux chevaux* he needs a woman if ever a man did and she'd tell him put your fork down Colin put your fork down . . .'

I was caught like a fly in a web. How was I ever to escape? This could go on forever. No one had supplied Fernande with punctuation. No one had ever given her commas or full stops for Christmas.

At that moment Fernande took off her glasses and absentmindedly cleaned them, putting them down on the table in front of her. I knew what to do. Steal them. This was a cruel thing to do to a distinguished lady. I was ashamed. But to hell with it. It was me or her. Not that sudden darkness interrupted the soliloquy.

'Now where did I put my glasses oh dear oh dear what have I done with my spectacles now calm down Fernande don't go thinking that you're off your rocker dear take things in their stride worse things can happen think of Edouard my dear brother Edouard who spends the best part of his time would you believe it staring out of the window of his oven of a flat counting the birds on the telegraph wires what a way to spend your life one two three he goes jotting them down on a piece of paper whoops did I tread on the cat poor sod . . .'

As she chattered on, I stood up and tiptoed out to rejoin Lou in the kitchen. 'What are you doing?' I asked.

Lou was at the sink wearing rubber gloves. 'The washing up. Fernande is *bordélique*.'

'Why did you leave me alone with her?'

'*Y'a un un lézard?*'

A lizard. Why is she talking about lizards?

She translated. 'Is there a problem?'

'She never stops talking. She's driving me round the bend.'

'You left her all by herself?'

'Yes.'

'But she's still talking!'

'I stole her glasses.'

This confession blurted out in front of someone who had wasted her misspent youth in the arms of a provincial optician was tantamount to blasphemy. I put the boot in.

'Your optician would never do that, of course?!'

Lou looked aghast. 'My optician? What the hell are you talking about?'

The parrot on my shoulder tried to dissuade me, chirping, 'Cool, Mikaël.' But I've never heeded parrots.

I told her, 'You think I can't see what's going on? You spend your exotic holidays harpooning fish with Mortier. You use *me* for visiting your delightful but nutty family.'

'You're paranoid.'

'I'm English.' This didn't seem to be particularly logical but it sounded sharp.

'Give her back her glasses immediately.'

'You even sound like him!!'

'*T'es complètement barjo.*'

I'd never heard *barjo* before but I got the gist. She screwed a finger into her forehead.

'You're out of your tiny mind! *C'est pas vrai!*'

Retreat seemed to be the order of the day so I rejoined Fernande.

'. . . funny you hear noises I was certain I heard the salon door open but my hearing's going as well I remember on the Ile de Bréhat when we were all on holiday it must have been twenty years ago suddenly in the middle of the night . . .'

All in all it took Fernande about two and half hours

to wind down. Around three o'clock she started to show signs of fatigue. The syntax stuttered, you could chip in with the odd question, and a remark and – *ô miracle* – just before four o'clock I managed to compose a whole sentence.

Lou and I drove back to Tours in silence. This was our first tiff. *Notre premier tiff? Nous avons tiffé?* It didn't sound terribly French. But I didn't dare ask.

A letter from Ariane awaited in the red letterbox at Toison. A letter and an invitation to the wedding of her niece. Last year she invited me to a fancy-dress party. I went as Margaret Thatcher, but I was the only guest in disguise. This time Ariane sought forgiveness. I just had to experience a real French wedding. *Tu dois ab-so-lu-ment être des nôtres. Je t'en supplie. S'il te plaît*, she wrote.

Maï-quel was delighted to accept.

15

Bip bip. The sound of a small French horn – by which I do not, of course, mean a French horn. It was Bernard the postman in his yellow van. One could hardly expect him to announce his arrival by playing Mozart in B flat.

Bernard was delighted. He brought good tidings! *Bip bip.* I was invited to the Tricot wedding. *Bip bip.* The blessing was to be given by le Père Chausson, one of the region's best blessers. Good job it wasn't le Père Jules. It was going to be a very classy do. *Le chic du chic.*

How the hell did he know all this before I'd even opened the envelope? Bernard winked a special postman's wink, then let me into a professional secret. He hoisted a small halogen torch from the bottom of his satchel. Postman's wink number two. You hold the envelope up to the light, shine the torch at it, and lo and behold, you can read what's inside! His function rendered the torch essential. A lot of people on his country round were elderly. Bad news could give them a heart-attack. Thanks to his trusty torch, Bernard could prepare the ground with a few well-chosen words. 'Last time I saw Pierre he wasn't looking too hot,' that kind of thing. That's what public service was all about. *Bip bip.* And off he went.

Ariane's invitation I had accepted purely on anthropological grounds. What exactly was *un mariage à la française*? I bought a small reporter's notebook and slipped it into the pocket of my linen suit. I wore a floppy Panama for the total Englishman look and a large striped tie, purchased during the *Semaine anglaise* at the local Centre Leclerc, guaranteed machine washable, which would serve both as a reminder of my Oxford past and, in the event of hasty eating, as a Terylene napkin.

On the hill overlooking the village of Paulmy, local inhabitants had been dragooned into dressing up as peasants to serve as parking attendants, directing elegantly dressed wedding guests into the mud. Wonderfully decorative hats – an ostrich nest? the summit of Mont Blanc complete with a rubbish bin? – were almost unmanageable in the wind whipping down between two corrugated iron silos. A young lady in front of me had problems both with hat and skirt and decided, much to our delight, to dedicate herself solely to her hat.

Once inside the nave I didn't know where to sit. The gleaming teeth of the guests on the left indicated the presence of a delegation of dentists from Loches and I decided to join them. On each rickety chair and on each worm-eaten pew a programme, with two doves giving each other a smacker on the cover, announced the order of events. Most of it was in Latin and I hadn't brought a dictionary. So I followed the movement instead – when in Rome etc – which proved none too easy. Some stood, some sat, a handful got down on the floor, the rest yo-yo'd.

The Abbé Chausson was togged out in a classy chasuble and, like Cedric Pinson, a pair of leather flip-flops. The harmonium proved a shade asthmatic, which in no way unsettled the full-bosomed contralto, whose talents were graphically illustrated during the tremolos of Gounod's *Ave Maria*.

The sermon was made incomprehensible by the amplification system, specially installed for the purposes by Ultra Son, from Descartes. A word would leave Father Chausson's lips, fly up into the vaulted ceiling, bounce off an ornate cornice, and fall to the floor to shatter into tiny pieces. In order to understand you'd have to pick up the bits and stick them back together again.

No need to hire the services of a professional photographer. Every second someone would leap up from their pew and brandish their mobile in the direction of the altar – an activity which engendered an immediate flurry of discussion.

'*C'est le nouveau Samsung.*'

'*Plutôt le Nokia, non?*'

The uncle of the groom had the latest BlackBerry and was sending a live video of the service to a colleague in Shanghai.

A trumpet sounded. Handel accompanied us out of the church on to the forecourt, where a guard of honour formed by swarthy men in livery from the local hunt prepared to sound their horns in honour of the bride and groom. Amongst them was the trusty Claudius who had served the family for generations and who had insisted on leaving his hospital bed where he was recovering from a stroke. Very red in the face, Claudius was carted off to the café for a Badoit and a fag.

The pack had also been invited. Iago, a spotty dog with a long tongue, made a fool of himself by eating a cat. Naughty Iago. We all walked back up the hill in the cheeky wind to get into our cars and to drive off to the reception. The red Mazda was out of place in the flotilla of more classy limousines but I had taken steps to blend in. On the rear bumper of the car I had tied one or two empty tins – one of *cassoulet* and another of *petits pois extra fins*. From time to time I sounded the horn and flashed the warning lights on and off. The cars in front of me frowned. But I knew the ropes. This was how we celebrated weddings in Toison.

The venue for the reception was a castle that had been destroyed during the Revolution of 1789 and rebuilt at the beginning of the twentieth century by an industrialist from Brittany who had made his fortune in salt cod. It now housed le Musée de la Pomme de Terre – a spud museum open to the public five days a week and containing the world's largest collection of rare tubercules. The Paulmy peasants had preceded us and once again inveigled the smart set to park in the mud.

A jazz band welcomed us in the courtyard composed of a cashier from the Crédit Agricole in Descartes, a plumber from Ligueil, two amateur firemen from Perrusson, and an assistant from Bricorama on the drums. The apéritif served on the castle lawns in full view of the world's largest potato patch, was sumptuous: prawns jumped in a wok, *foie gras* on warm bread, and all kinds of oysters. The only false note was a secondhand *belon* oyster, whose condition only struck me on the point of swallowing. Pretending to sneeze, I slipped it into a handy Kleenex.

Ariane, wearing a hat which looked like a peacock with an erection, appeared behind me. Sensing the danger, I quickly slipped oyster and Kleenex into my pocket.

'Maï-quel.'

'Ah! Ariane.'

She slipped her arm under mine and squeezed. '*Viens, Maï-quel*. Take me to the potatoes.'

Fortunately, at that moment the band struck up 'When the Saints Go Marching In', announcing the beginning of dinner. *Ouf*. Saved by the bell.

Under the awning of the huge circus-style tent was a blackboard and easel on which were pinned the seating arrangements. My fellow guests on the *Forget-Me-Not* table? An estate agent from the swish *16ième arrondissement* in Paris whose hobby was big-game hunting in Africa, an editor of schoolbooks on the point of going bust, a one-time model who was now doing charity work with ex-miners in the North, and a gentleman who had the Ferrari franchise in Saudi Arabia, where he'd just made a killing. In my endeavour to please I confused things, discussing miners with the sports car professional, killing rhinos with the depressed publisher and Ferraris with the sexy social worker.

The acoustics of the tent were as bad as those of the church, the canvas proving far more absorbing than the conversation. It was difficult to understand anything. Tent French is even more unfathomable than the normal variety. I managed to make out that the table were discussing toothbrushes. Have you tried to buy a toothbrush recently? They are now all made in ridiculous shapes. The handle gaudy and twisted, the bristle an absurdly bright colour. We all regretted the passing of the traditional brush. Shoes no longer look like shoes. Toothbrushes no longer look like toothbrushes. Where was civilization heading?

I was disconcerted to discover that everyone around the table seemed to be suffering from a disease about which, until then, I had heard nothing. The new scourge was the ISF and they'd all got it. The outbreak was particularly severe in the smart quarters of Paris. I decided to wash my hands between courses as a precautionary measure. Rather silly because the disease turned out to be the *Impôt Sur la Fortune*. The tax on the rich.

In order to relax after the exhaustion of the *badinage*, I slipped away into the darkness of the spud museum, only to be joined by a lithe Ariane who must have spotted my diversionary tactics.

'You came alone, Maï-quel?'

'Oh no, Ariane. No. Lou was to come but at the last minute she couldn't,' I lied.

'Being unfaithful to our little schoolteacher?'

'She is an *agrégée*, Ariane.'

'*How* exciting.'

Elle se moque.

'Look, Maï-quel!' Ariane pointed to the penumbral potatoes. 'Just look. They have such extraordinary shapes!'

She giggled and squeezed my hand. 'Just look at that one! Now what does *that* remind you of?'

Ariane's dirty botany was interrupted by the vibrations of the disco. In the distant tent the guests were waving their napkins above their heads like the blades of a helicopter, chanting, '*Une chan-son! Une chan-son!*'

Ariane gave me a sly wink. '*A tout à l'heure*, Maï-quel. See you at the fireworks.'

A queue had formed in front of the chic, military-style field loos, looking like a series of opaque telephone boxes. Father Chausson, confused no doubt by the pictograms, his chasuble and the amount of Vouvray he had tucked away behind it, was seen staggering out

of the Ladies. From inside the tent the DJ invited us
to bop. To the tune of 'That's When My Heartache
Begins' Dick Rivers, the great 1960s French rocker,
sang: *'Sous le ciel écossais . . ./Là, on pourra s'aimer.'*

The dancefloor was invaded by pensioners, who
remembered the song, and by children under three, who
liked it. Sciatica and angina were thrown to the winds.
Let's twist again like we did last summer . . .

We were then all invited to traipse up to the top
of the hill overlooking the valley, ladies collecting a
shawl or a warm blanket on the way. The firework
display awaited. In the dark of the path I was struck by
a curious premonition. There was a large hibiscus on
my left. No one was looking. I took the Kleenex and
the dead oyster out of my pocket and threw them under
the fronds. *Be prepared*, I thought. Lord Baden Powell,
who would never have dreamed of finding himself
in the situation I foresaw, would have been both
impressed and appalled.

The pyrotechnics began. Each golden shower, every
Roman Candle, each and every celestial Catherine-
wheel was greeted with rapturous applause. The fireworks made me think of Emmeline, Emmeline of Lou.
I felt ashamed. With reason. I sensed Ariane's perfume
behind me. I knew that her body was close to mine in
the dark. I knew what was going to happen.

'Maï-quel . . .'

This was not our first French kiss. But at the barbecue party at the Château de la Souche, a chipolata
sausage I had carelessly left lingering in my jacket
pocket had put a sudden end to our ardent, erotic
encounter. This time my pockets had been emptied of
encumbering objects. As her lips met mine I saw Lou
Charpin's key in the doorway of Château Mortier,

Boulevard Bérenger. I saw the optician triumphant in the tropical swimming pool astride his inflatable Quad.

Vengeance is sweet.

The final tableau lit up the night sky. From behind us, the jazz band accompanied the entry of the *pièce montée* – the traditional wedding cake – a vast pyramid of caramelized *choux à la crème*. As Ariane slipped away into the night, I returned, my eyes sparkling, my mind spinning, to the table and to the toothbrushes . . .

16

Rubbish – *les ordures ménagères* – is a headache in the country.

In the good old days, the entry into the village was heralded by two containers surrounded by a hedge of dead thuyas. In the green bin you dumped bottles, in the blue bin everything else. This division proved too regimental for the anarchic French. The village redesigned the system. According to one's mood, some rubbish was considered suitable for the left-hand container and other rubbish for the right-hand container. We would meet in the thuya enclave and pass the time of day exercising our right to be pig-headed. In the France of Louis XIV they'd had the salons; until recently in Toison we'd had the bins.

Times had changed. Rationalization had taken over. Nowadays we put our rubbish in black plastic bin bags which are deposited at the end of our drives to be collected once a week by a team of dustmen who, like the Flying Dutchman, pass mysteriously and silently on their nocturnal errand. This system was much to the delight of the dogs. Aimé Matou's horde undid the bags with great dexterity, and decorated the adjoining fields and hedgerows with used Kleenex boxes and yoghurt pots. To dissuade them, tidy house-owners had taken to building wooden slatted containers at the bottom of the drive and storing the bags in there. Some had even purchased their own bins and personalized them with geraniums, china rabbits and French-style dwarves – Droopy smoking a Gauloise. Auguste Renard had purchased at Castorama a fibro-cement reproduction of the Venus de Milo which he had artfully positioned so it looked as if the statue was searching for her arms in his bin. This was generally considered to be pretentious.

The personal bin posed another problem. Those who couldn't be bothered to build their own container or buy a new dustbin threw their bags into other people's bins. These criminals were referred to as the 'cuckoos'. You'd wake up in the morning and discover your private bin choc-à-bloc with other people's muck – leaving no place for your own. A vigilante group had been formed to roam the canton at night on cuckoo watch.

Not particularly gifted in the handyman department, I stood at the bottom of the drive dreaming of what I might have constructed. The French for a container is *une benne*. I fantasized about a bin in the shape of the Houses of Parliament which I would have called 'Big Benne'. My musings were interrupted by the arrival of Laurent, Lou's brother, in his dusty VW Golf with its *I ♥ Bulgaria* stickers. He was pale and feverish, his dark-ringed eyes darting glances left and right as if he was in danger of being discovered doing something he shouldn't. His suit was creased. Gisèle kept him very dapper and tidy. Maybe he hadn't been home for a few days?

He hailed me, came in for a coffee, sat down on the terrace and spilled the beans. The problem was simple.

'*J'ai le feu au cul, mon vieux.*'

A future brother-in-law who arrives in a cloud of

dust to inform you that his backside is on fire might at first be thought a little disconcerting – but I was prepared. I had heard the expression before. Laurent had whispered the confession to me at table during the Christmas meal at l'Allée Notre Dame. As he had his back to the hearth I immediately suggested he change places. I hadn't understood the metaphor.

'For you English, it's not the same,' he had explained. 'You can't understand. For us Latins, it's in our genes. There's nothing we can do about it.'

Laurent was the ultimate *chaud lapin* – the hot rabbit in person. A sex maniac and proud of it. He took out his laptop.

'I'll show you my collection,' he said hoarsely.

He'd brought his stamps?

Double click. Laurent pointed to the screen. A long list of names, addresses, vital statistics, favourite restaurants, political leanings and taste in underwear. A hard disk harem.

'Not forgetting their *truc*.'

Truc? Thing?

He clicked on *truc*.

'You know, dressing up in a nurse's uniform with a whip.'

Why would you need a whip in a hospital? I had no time to put the question.

'I must examine the house,' he announced suddenly, and went upstairs. The bedding was on the hard side. If ever I wanted to change it, he'd a friend at *L'Univers du Sommeil*. He went in one Tuesday to test a new Dunlopillo latex and didn't leave until Thursday morning. Wink wink. The window in the gable end was useful, apparently.

'For a quick escape.' Nudge. 'You never know!'

The rustic rosewood wardrobe was just what the doctor ordered. The bane of his life? DIY. The world is populated with inadequate husbands. Instead of taking care of their hungry, sensual wives they spend their weekends assembling Swedish wardrobes with the help of a plan in Estonian and a cruciform screwdriver.

'You're in bed relaxing after a strenuous afternoon when she cries, "*Ciel, mon mari!*" On with your trousers. Too late to run downstairs. Where to hide? Only one solution. In the wardrobe. You jump in and – *boum* – the whole thing falls apart. *Fait chier, Ikea!*'

He looked at me pleadingly.

'So. You'll lend it to me?'

The wardrobe?

'The house.'

I hesitated. Not so Laurent.

'*Merci, vieux*. You know what you are?'

A coward?

'A brother.'

'And what about Gisèle?'

'Gisèle? What's it got to do with Gisèle? She's my wife, *vieux*.'

The logic was implacable. Laurent was already dreaming of the blissful afternoons to come. The present woman of his life was Anna Pavlovna, the principal violin of the Lyrica Bulgarica, the orchestra invited to Loches for the summer opera festival. *Ah, la Pavlovna*! The merest caress of her bow on a taut string was enough to bring tears to his eyes. In the meantime he might use the house from time to time, 'Just to keep in trim.'

And so, two or three times a week, Laurent would

transform the cottage into a den of vice. He told Gisèle he was folding programmes. In truth I'd do the folding and he the unfolding. Having no desire to hang around as he put his fire out, I'd go down to the bottom of the garden for a chinwag with the leeks. The noises coming from upstairs were at times so intrusive I took to singing Johnny Hallyday out loud:

Que je t'ai-me,
Que je t'aime
Que t'aime
Que je t'aimmmmeeee etc.'

A little on the repetitive side but apposite. The leeks thought I was barmy.

Then, suddenly, what the gods had designed to happen, came to pass. Laurent phoned.

'You do have central heating?' he asked.

Could his backside suddenly have gone cold? I reassured him.

'Génial!'

He was going to pop in on Tuesday, he told me, to fold a few programmes with Élodie, an accountant from Cussay. *Son truc?*

'She likes being tied to radiators!'

By this time, after Jean-Claude and the broom cupboard, I was blasé.

Tuesday came. While Laurent and Elodie disappeared upstairs, I took a stroll down the drive to avoid the sardonic remarks of my vegetables. The evening was warm, a heron was gliding high in the sky over the lake beyond the Matou farmhouse. My temporary banishment had a good side to it. Lost in my pastoral contemplations I was almost run over by Eric Moineau, the *plombier électricien*, who arrived in his white van. He gave me a big electric smile.

'You must be pleased to see me, Monsieur Sadler!'

'You're telling me, Eric. *Et comment!*' I had been phoning him ever since February.

'*Eh bien*. Today's the day. We're going to fix them at last!'

'Fix what?' It had been so long, I'd forgotten what the problem was!

'*Les gargouillements, pardi!*'

'What gurgling?'

'*Dans les radiateurs.*'

The smile froze on my face. Not the radiators. No, not now!

'*Non, non, Monsieur Moineau*. There's no need. *Plus besoin. Ça marche. Ça va!*'

Try saying *ça ne gargouille plus* when you're het up! I started to gurgle myself. But there was no point in protesting. Eric Moineau stuck to his guns.

'*On va les purger, les radiateurs!*'

My protests were in vain. The van was already speeding up the path under the compassionate eyes of the Matou herd. I remained disconsolate at the bottom of the drive. What else could I do? Nothing but wait for the return of the plumber. Which was quick to happen. After three or four minutes the white van came speeding back down the drive. Eric Moineau wound down the window and looked at me in disgust. He was pale.

'Monsieur Sadler.' There was a quiet hurt in his voice.

'Monsieur Moineau?'

'*Je vous ai pris en flagrant délit.*' I have caught you red-handed.

Oh dear.

'You have turned to another plumber.'

'*Non, vraiment, Monsieur Moineau – ce n'est pas un autre plombier.*'

'I have heard the banging. I have heard the grunting. You have only to put your ear to the pipes.'

Heaven forbid.

'Monsieur Sadler. Someone else is purging in my place.'

You can say that again, Eric.

'That is disloyal, Monsieur Sadler.'

Suddenly, in the distance, from upstairs came a terrible ecstatic cry.

'*OUI OUI OUI . .* '

'You hear, Monsieur Sadler? The plumber has solved the problem.' Monsieur Moineau paused and then, with a truly Cornelian sense of tragedy, put the knife in the wound. 'You have made one plumber happy. You have made another plumber sad.'

And he was gone.

Ever since then whenever I am awoken by gurgling in the central heating system in the middle of the night, I think of Gisèle, then I think of Laurent, then of Anna Pavlovna, then of infidelity, then of Lou, then of Mortier, then of Mauritius, then of vanilla pods, then of the Nouvelle Vague. And only then do I manage to get back to sleep again.

17

In France, the SNCF, the National Railway System, has always been associated with the Resistance. During the Second World War railwaymen bravely derailed trains, exploded signal boxes and generally caused patriotic havoc. The most recent manifestation of railway resistance, however, was causing me more pain than admiration.

Sylvie took me aside in the garden. There was a terrible family secret she had to divulge, she whispered. She looked around. No one was hiding behind the trees. There were no dwarves with microphones in the bushes.

'It's Rémi,' she told me. She blushed and, biting her tongue, blurted it out. *'Rémi est coco.'*

A green bean?

'Un coco. Un rouge.' Seeing my incomprehension, she leaned forward and hissed, *'C'est un communiste.'*

Poor Sylvie was in tears. They'd tried everything: a year's subscription to *Le Figaro*, a week in la Baule, a pink Lacoste polo shirt, half-moon spectacles worn on a ribbon around his neck, a Ralph Lauren shirt. In vain. Nothing doing. *Rien à faire.* It was indelible.

A visit to his garden confirmed the diagnosis. Behind the vegetable patch with its giant carrots – he considered that 'bio' was bourgeois – Rémi had built a breezeblock replica of Lenin's tomb equipped with an electric pump. For the anniversary of the October Revolution the fountain gushed red wine. The box hedge had been cut into a topiary hammer and sickle.

Sylvie detested this garden. For family do's she would cover the hedge and the mausoleum with a plastic sheet. She also loathed the way that Rémi affected a working-class vocabulary and accent. He said *barbaque* instead of *viande* and over-accentuated his circumflex accents – saying *châââteau* instead of *château*. He had been so clever at school. Was it such a heinous crime to be middle-class? Sylvie served herself a slug of consolatory rosé.

Rémi considered me to be an unacceptable product of post-Thatcherite Britain. Serious steps had to be taken to win him over. OK, he was the black sheep of the family, but his vote counted. I'd lent my radiators to Laurent. I'd sat with a parrot on my head in Boussay. Rémi was next on the list.

An opportunity came with an invitation to an SNCF retirement party in the left-wing stronghold of St Pierre des Corps. Lou couldn't go and I stepped into her shoes. Like an actor, I prepared for the role. I read the Communist Party Manifesto once bought in a Save the Kangaroo jumble sale in Abesbury along with *Cooking without Cream* and *Health through Seaweed*. I learned the words of the 1936 Front Populaire anthem '*Le Temps des Cerises*'. Calling people *camarade* didn't come naturally, so I practised while shaving and rehearsed when buying bread in Toison.

'*Merci, camarade*,' I smiled.

Madame Roubaud was well-known for being a radical leftie and stone deaf.

To get in the mood I travelled from Tours to St Pierre des Corps – which has voted Communist since 1920 –

by train, the so-called *navette*. The bourgeois archi-
tecture of the affluent provincial capital quickly gave
way to the ravages of collectivization: back gardens full
of abandoned machinery, rusting clothes-poles, cheap
broken toys, piles of wood to be eked out through the
long winters, vegetable plots. The journey was fast and
cheap. Three minutes for 1.80 Euros. Paris to Moscow
at a knockdown price.

At St Pierre the station buffet was a disappointment.
No large jars of cucumber in vinegar, no samovars,
and no queues of babushkas with string bags waiting
for the long-promised arrival of oranges. Things looked
up when I glanced down Avenue Stalingrad – the
name itself brought a flush to my cheeks. The avenue
was wide and empty, clearly awaiting the arrival of the
jubilant masses celebrating the failure of the potato
crop. In 1967 the Russian astronaut Titov had visited
St Pierre in person. He had greeted the townsfolk from
the balcony of the Hôtel de Ville, after which he left
to inaugurate a crossroads between two tower blocks.
This had since been named in his honour Le Carrefour
des Cosmonautes. I stood on the spot getting a Soviet
buzz. I was ripe for the party.

Rémi's colleagues, waiting on platform 7, eyed me
with some suspicion – not surprising in the presence
of a representative of a country where, according to
recent statistics, 14 per cent of trains which leave never
arrive. A grey and orange diesel locomotive pulled into
the station adorned with a large banner announcing,
Son dernier train. Dédé, the future OAP, descended
from the cabin to the applause of his friends and family.
We had a group photograph taken leaning against
the buffers.

The party was held in a prefab belonging to the CGT

standing in amongst a labyrinth of tracks near a signal box called *Les Epines fortes*. Inside, the walls had been papered with a panoramic view of the Alps. On the Formica trestle tables were piles of plastic cups and plates wrapped in cellophane. A large red-faced lady was opening packets of Chipsters using her teeth as scissors. We were each offered a Kir Royal – crème de cassis and warm Vouvray pétillant. There'd been a power failure and the fridge didn't work.

When the guests hung their smart Sunday best *bleu de travail* on the hooks I once again felt out of place. I didn't have the regulation SNCF morphology. The British who drink beer and eat crisps and milk chocolate boast a belly which starts just under the chin and describes a graceful arc, tailing off at the toes. The French store excess baggage in a different fashion. Their gut is more camel-like, a sudden and often unexpected hump, like a rucksack worn backwards, adorning a body which seems not to have been designed to support such a weighty protuberance. The vertical position must require a good deal of balance. The room was quite small. As they walked around, their stomachs would bump one against the other, making the noise of two taut Hollofil cushions colliding. Clearly they were very fond of them. I caught them in unguarded moments stroking their gut as if it were a pet animal.

To attract our attention, the *chef de gare* knocked his Swiss penknife against a bottle of pastis 51 and took a wad of notes from his inside pocket. He retraced Dédé's career, decorated him with the Long Service Medal and presented him with his farewell presents: an electric border-cutter for his garden, an encyclopaedia, a cheque and a huge bouquet of extremely long-stemmed upright roses for his wife whose *mise en plis* made her look like a CRS wearing a fancifully decorated helmet.

The *cassis* ran out and was replaced by *mûres* (black-berry liqueur) but no one seemed to *kir*. I had no one to tell my joke to and tried to catch Rémi's eye. In vain. He was clearly giving me the cold shoulder. He and his colleagues were huddled around a large table in the far corner. The discussion was hushed and intense. For the first time in my life I was party to the meeting of a cell, a kind of coven minus the cauldron. Difficult to know quite how to position myself. To keep my distance could be read as an ideological aloofness, as if I was cutting myself off from the masses. On the other hand, drawing up a chair and joining in could also be misinterpreted. I might be a Blairist spy dispatched to uncover the plotting of the militant left.

The group was compact and impenetrable. Notes were being scribbled down, statistics exchanged. I caught scraps of their conversation – the odd figure: 2.5; 4. They must be percentages or swings; they were probably analysing election results. I'd done my home-work. I knew the plight of the Left. After the golden era of the 1950s the PCF had lost support. I began to hum an upbeat version of the *'Internationale'* but no one could give a hoot.

A passing gut grazed by. *'Pardon, camarade.'*

The discussion became more intense. More statistics were thrown out. *'23!'*

I couldn't believe my ears. Twenty-three per cent? If they were talking about their chances in the next elections they'd have another think coming. They were taking, as the vernacular would have it, *leurs vessies pour des lanternes* – their bladders for lanterns.

'That must have been in 1936,' I declared.

The group stopped at the sound of my voice. 1936? Why was the *rosbif* suddenly talking about the *Front populaire*? They looked at each other. *Il est fou ou quoi?* They turned their backs and got on with their business. Suddenly, a comrade pulled something out of his bag. At last. It must be a *tract* – a hand-out for the next march. Workers of the world, unite!

'*Dis donc la Comtesse,*' I heard next. The countess? I identified the age-old loathing of the aristocracy. It dated back to the Revolution. The guillotine was not a thing of the past.

'23.5!'

Could that be her score? Was the countess standing in the elections? Rémi took a little red book out of his pocket. Readings from Chairman Mao? I leaned forward.

'One portion of foie gras sausages Comtesse du Barry. 250 grammes. 23.5 points.'

What the . . .?

'And the *cassoulet*?'

'22.'

Re-merde. This was not a hotbed of revolution. This was a meeting of Weight Watchers. That wasn't a Marxist pamphlet. That was a non-stick sheet for frying without fat. The Comtesse du Barry was not a class enemy. It was the trade name of a company specialising in goose *charcuterie*. They were not fighting capitalism. They were fighting fat.

I went outside to get a breath of fresh air. The sun was setting behind the giant power station. A TGV was picking up speed as it left for Montparnasse. I gave a disconsolate kick at the ballast. *Je suis con.* I must give up pretending to be someone I'm not. Stop trying to please everyone all the time.

Changeons notre fusil d'épaule. Let's put our gun on the other shoulder. Change tactics.

18

A postcard from Richard Badger, erstwhile Head of Department at the University of Swindon, the academic greaser who drove a new Porsche and thought France was old hat. The picture was of a country-style wedding and the message one laconic word on the back.

Alors?

True, my rash refectory announcement was slow to materialize. Lou was not quick to conquer, one day blowing hot, the next blowing cold. I had to put my house in order, take the bull by the horns and get my finger out.

An opportunity to test the new Michael was quick to present itself. In deep conversation with the leeks, I noticed my neighbour Aimé Matou loitering around the haunch of a buxom cow in the neighbouring field.

Since my success of the preceding year in the village garden festival, Aimé and I had not been on friendly terms. True, I had been sly. He was the more accomplished gardener, but he was less cunning. Rearranging my vegetable patch in the middle of the night to spell out *Vive la France* in leeks was, even if I say it myself, a stroke of genius. Our relations had been further strained by the presence of one of his dwarf hens, whom I called Mildred, who would sleep all day in the forsythia and wreak havoc in the tomatoes at night. All well and good. But when the bitch started to make lacework of my turnips, I'd had enough. I picked up a large stone and was on the point of turning Mildred into *pâté de poule* when I saw Aimé out of the corner of my eye. I pretended to be practising cricket rather than decimating poultry, but he was not to be taken in.

Could this be an end to the hostilities? Were we going to be friends again?

It was out of the question that Aimé should make any move in my direction. Peasant etiquette forbids any ardent manifestation of a desire for communication. I therefore stepped over the electric fence – taking great care to avoid jeopardizing my undercarriage – and walked determinedly through the herd who, true to form, did not even bat an eyelash and looked the udder way.

Arriving some ten yards from Aimé I then enacted surprise: *'Tiens, Aimé!'* As if we had bumped into each other on Regent's Street.

Aimé gave his cap a one centimetre push up his brow to reveal a beady eye and nodded infinitesimally. Clearly he was delighted to see me.

'Il fait chaud,' I remarked conversationally.

'Pardi.'

Not the most striking opening exchange, but *marivaudage* with Aimé tends to be sluggish. I pursued.

'Pour la saison.'

'Pardi.'

Having exhausted that item of conversation, Aimé redirected the cloud of flies which had gathered around to listen to the sparkling badinage. I sensed he had something to tell me so decided to bide my time, keeping close guard on his mouth like a journalist waiting for white smoke to emerge from a Vatican chimney. Suddenly the message came.

'*Dimanche.*'

In itself, 'Sunday' is a somewhat elliptical utterance. It could be the beginning of the weather forecast. It might be the first line in a poem by Mallarmé. As he didn't venture any more information, I decided to press the matter.

'*Dimanche?*'

From the depths of the well he hauled a sentence to the surface. '*Dimanche on tue le cochon.*'

I was moved to tears. Aimé was inviting me to a party. I suddenly felt as if I belonged to the community. It was as if I had received an embossed card.

> *Monsieur Aimé Matou*
> *At Home*
> *RSVP*
> *Casual dress.*

Full of myself, I went down to the village, but the Toison d'Or gang were not ready to share my enthusiasm. The Tasmalou turned their backs, sulking. I was hurt. 'What had I done?' I asked. No one replied. If they continued to carry on in this way, I said, I would confiscate their Zimmer frames. So, they spilled the beans.

'*On n'est pas assez bien, hein?*'

Of course they were presentable.

'*On est des bouseux? Des ploucs?*'

No, they weren't yokels. No, they weren't bumpkins.

'*Tu nous la caches, la petite?*'

The truth dawned. Long ago I had promised to introduce them to Lou, but I'd never come up trumps. I implored their pardon. I would make amends. Settle accounts and cheer them up. Two stones with one bird. They beamed. On Sunday, I declared, Mademoiselle

Charpin would accompany me to the *fête chez Aimé.*
Promis juré.

'*Faut quand même qu'on la voïye,*' said Henri, using
a special and totally incorrect subjunctive to emphasize
the importance of the moment.

We were all invited to *tuer le cochon.* This, I
presumed, was yet another of those colourful French
animal metaphors of which my vocabulary book was
full: *avoir du chien* (to have some dog) = to be v. classy;
faire un bœuf (to do an ox) = to do a jam session; *un
coup vache* (a cow blow) = a dirty trick; *un remède de
cheval* (a horse remedy) = stiff medicine. I was unable
to find *tuer le cochon* in the dictionary – always pretty
unhelpful when it comes to argot – but I eventually
figured it out. *Cochon* is what you call someone when
they show themselves to be sex-mad.

'*J'aime bien ta petite jupette dans le vent, Madeleine.*'
'*Cochon!*'

'Killing the pig' must mean something like 'control-
ling one's sex-drive'. It was doubtless a country ritual,
with the equivalent of Morris dancers and maypoles,
celebrating the attainment of wisdom once the storm
of adolescence has passed. A kind of post-libido Bar
Mitzvah.

This was the kind of invitation Lou would go for.
She loved the country, having spent her school holidays
on a farm learning to reverse caravans. I told her she
was in for a treat but kept the details secret. If he knew,
Mortier would cringe, I gloated.

The great day arrived. I parked the Mazda behind the
Tasmalou flotilla moored in front of Aimé's dank pond.
A dirty duck immediately sat on the bonnet in order to
warm its behind. Hens were queuing up to lay their

eggs in the remains of a Renault 4. The Matou horde rushed out to greet us and started eating my trousers. It was all delightfully authentic. Thierry would have been thrilled.

Noise was coming from the courtyard. When we turned the corner we were faced with a scene straight out of a Breughel painting. A vast pig had been attached to an old concrete telegraph pole and had been hoisted into a position as if for a Black Mass crucifixion. The Tasmalou were gathered around the carcass. Pois-Chiche and Henri were passing a burning torch over its gut while Roger and Nestor were meticulously shaving it using two blue Bic twin-blade sensitive skin razors.

'But, what's that?' I asked, aghast.

'*C'est le cochon.*'

'What cochon?'

'*Le cochon qu'on vient de tuer, pardi.*'

My world collapsed. I had been stupidly metaphorical. *Tuer le cochon* meant just what it said. A shade less romantic than I had imagined. I was pale. Not so Aimé Matou, who seemed delighted to see me. Clearly I had arrived at the right moment.

'*Ah, le Maïkèle, . . . le Maïkèle!*'

Le Maïkèle was slightly less fulsome but concealed his reticence. I was keen to introduce Lou.

'*Bonjour, Aimé . . . Oui, ça fait longtemps que je voulais vous présenter . . .*'

But Aimé had no time for niceties.

'*Tenez!*' He gave me a large saucepan – *un faitout* – to hold and placed it and me next to the smouldering beast.

'*On y va.*'

He took a large knife from the pocket of his overall. I turned, looking desperately for Lou.

'*Deux secondes, Lou, je—*'

With a savage gesture Aimé sunk his knife into the pig's neck. Blood spurted out like oil from a geyser.

'*Attention! Le faitout!*'

I had to perform a dance of death around the poor pig to catch the stuff. It was gold dust. The Tasmalou gave the animal a big shake to extract the last drops and took the saucepan out of my hands. At last I could get on with the introductions. Or I could have done, if it hadn't been for Aimé.

'*Maintenant passons aux choses sérieuses.*'

There was worse to come?

Aimé positioned me in front of the gut of the epilated pig. He then gave me a large tin bath. There was a terrible gleam in his eye. This was the moment he had been waiting for. Let's see what they were made of, *Les Angliches*. This'll teach 'em to fiddle with their leeks.

'*Accroche-toi, le Maïkele.*'

Like a murderous druid Aimé lifted a large gleaming knife. I didn't dare look. There was an appalling noise, like that made by a ton of dead squid falling from a great height on to a washboard. The noise of glurping and sloshing was accompanied by a overpowering stench of *merde*. Guts continued to tumble out in my bath. I considered passing out. This must be the *splanchnique* test. I should never have beaten Aimé in the garden competition.

I squinted pigwards. It seemed now to be quite empty. Aimé barked an order. I had to carry my bathful of steaming guts into the barn. I turned, hoping to catch Lou's eye.

'Won't be a mo', Lou,' I told her. 'I'll just deposit these intestines and . . .' Easier said than done to lug a ton of tripe across a farmyard pitted with crevices

full of slippery dung. I stumbled and some slimy pork
innards looking for all intents and purposes like hot
snot, fell into a cowpat.

'*Attention, le Maïkele!*'

All this was a terrible mistake. Mortier was scoring
an important point. The Ile Maurice, for all its boring
thatched huts, was more attractive than my offering.
But there was no time for reflexion.

'*Et maintenant, le Maïkele – le boudin!*'

Boudin! Not black sausagery! 'Mais—'. My protests
were unheeded. In fact, the more I protested, the more
he was delighted. First we had to prepare the *boyaux* –
the skins. This we did by blowing down long stretches
of gut to test that the bowels were not full of holes. This
I enjoyed as it reminded me of Christmas parties. Next
the blood. We plunged our hands into the bucket and
splashed around in order to eradicate any unwanted
lumps. A mixture of onions, fat in cubes and powdered
milk was then added. I suggested a slug of vodka to
make the world's most repulsive Bloody Mary but Aimé
was not in a laughing mood. A length of inflated bowel
– bowelling? – was attached to the end of a large funnel
and I was given the job of pushing the vile gunge out
into the sausage in order to fashion the *boudin*.

Aimé left. But not the cats and dogs who kept trying
to lick the mixture. To shoo them away, I threw bits
of fat at them which bounced back into the funnel – the
projectile thereby becoming an ingredient. The flies
were also in seventh heaven. From time to time an
obstreperous insect would get its feet stuck in the gunge
on the side of the bowl. It could no longer take off.
Thump! I gave it a clout with a rolled-up copy of the
guide culturel of the *Nouvelle République*. Splash –
it fell to an appalling death. After apple *boudin*, after

onion *boudin*, *enfin* the ultimate delicacy: fly *boudin*. I must put a sausage or two aside for Thierry.

But where was Lou? Had she left in disgust? Had she rung Mortier to tell him she'd made up her mind?

The barn door was ajar. Outside, the morning mist had begun to melt and the warm sun to encourage the birds to sing. The countryside came out of hiding, and unfolded like the backdrop to a painting by Poussin (or Chick if you insist on translation). In the middle of the courtyard was a vast steaming cauldron. Around it, Lou and the Tasmalou were stirring the *rillettes*, chatting and laughing. Lou plunged a wooden spoon into the bubbling magma, hauled it out covered in long-simmered pork and they cooled it, tasting, adding white wine, pepper and salt. *Quel professeur!*

It took them back to their schooldays, to the *certif* – the *certificat d'études*. They tried to catch each other out. The longest river? The largest capital? The formula for carbon dioxide? The agreement of the past participle? A train leaves Angoulême at eight o'clock travelling at 70 kilometres an hour and another leaves Tours at nine o'clock travelling at 80 kilometres an hour. Which one reaches Poitiers first? Lou replied with a grammatical mindbender. She asked them for the imperfect subjunctive of the verb *s'asseoir* – to sit down.

'*Que je m'asseyasse,*' said one.

They scratched their heads.

'*Oh, putain . . .*'

'*Que je m'assoisse.*'

Lou was wearing tight jeans and boots, her mass of black hair tied back by a red ribbon. The Tasmalou eyed her with expertise. They knew what they were looking for. For half a century, once a month at the cattle-market in Ligueil, they had learned to judge from afar: shank, pastern, fetlock, jaw. They approved. *Une belle bête, ma foi!* He knew what he was at, *le rosbif.* He'd stumbled on a gem. *Il avait déniché une perle.*

I was overcome with emotion. In order to admire Lou from my vantage-point in the barn I had to stop the flow of liquid *boudin.* I pulled a rickety chair towards me and lifted my leg, shoving the end of the funnel into the top of my boot. The funnel was now higher than the gunge. *Euréka,* the flow stopped. At that precise moment, the five friends, with their lined faces, decayed toothy smiles and their cracked old fingers held together by brown sellotape, broke into song – a song learned long ago behind their desks in the tiny primary school of Toison:

> *Colchiques dans les prés,*
> *Fleurissent, fleurissent . . .*

Henri caught sight of me in the dark of the barn. He raised his thumb. *Elle est top, la petite. Apte pour le service.* They gave their seal of approval. *Tu peux y aller, mon vieux.*

A moment of pure magic. Badger's challenge rang in my ears. Why wait any longer? Now was the time to pop the question. Now was the time to make my declaration. Bewitched, enchanted, moved, I forgot myself. I lowered my leg, removing my foot from the chair. The funnel was now lower than the gunge. The result was instantaneous. My boot filled with boudin.

'*Viens, le Maïkèle.*'

Bon Diou de bon Diou. What was I waiting for? It was no good being shy like Marcellin. I walked out into the glare of the courtyard. Splosh splosh.

'*C'est quoi, ce bruit?*'

Noise. What noise? I tried to disguise the liquid slopping in my boot. The sun highlighted her hair. A finch sang in the undergrowth. My colleagues from the University of Swindon stood around the cauldron waving their wedding presents. *Alors?* What was I waiting for?

'*Viens à côté de moi. Viens touiller.*' Come and stir.

I stood beside Lou, my welly close to the hot flames. '*Alors . . .*' I began.

The Tasmalou would help me out. They'd give me a hand with the subjunctives. *S'épouser?* To marry. *Il faut que nous nous épousions.* No, just a minute. No . . . *Épousassions.*

'*Alors?*' she replied.

I couldn't. The proximity of fire and cauldron began to take effect. The liquid *boudin* in my boot was cooking nicely. A slice of onion wedged itself between my toes. In no time my foot was encased in a mass of solidified black pudding.

The Tasmalou were dismayed but not surprised. Typical.

Trust a *rosbif* to chicken out.

19

The Tasmalou had a problem. Getting to the market in Ligueil on Mondays was no easy business. If you'd spent your life eating and drinking to the professional standards they had maintained, going up any slope was a struggle. Henri drove a very small car called a Matiz. Its top speed was 20 kilometres an hour and it could be driven without a licence – the only official qualification which Henri had ever met. He'd taken several runs at the hill out of Toison and the car, given the obvious disparity between size of engine and size of driver, petered out halfway up and ran ignominiously back down the village. Tubard owned a spotless 1972 Renault 14 that he was loath to take out of the garage for fear of scratching the paintwork – Ligueil was an asphalt jungle. There was only one other solution. *Le taxi anglais*. The trusty red Mazda.

The market was no longer what it used to be. The *charcutier* – the *roi du rillon* – had retired. The greengrocer had a hernia and could only serve baby carrots and cherry tomatoes. The cattle-market, held once a month, attracted the expert eye of the *paysans* who could still spot a wonky testicle a mile off. But the farmers were just playing a game. They'd sold out and moved into town, their land now owned by a retired Belgian industrialist who ran a *gîte*.

The high spot of the morning was their weekly trip to

get money out of the cash machine. For someone who, throughout his whole life, had kept his savings hidden under the mattress, or slipped between the sheets stored in the wardrobe, the invention was an aberration. Seeing your fortune broadcast to the world on a TV screen was financial exhibitionism.

The architects had carefully positioned it so that the midday sun shone directly on to the screen, making it unreadable. The Tasmalou made visors to shield their eyes out of the sturdy cardboard of *bouillie bordelaise* boxes – *bouillie bordelaise* is the copper sulphate solution which is the gardener's panacea, curing mildew, attacks by eagles and chicken pox. Unfortunately the *bouillie* in question is sticky and bright blue, and left large rings around their eyes, making the queue at the cash machine look like a glam rock band. Recently, a more efficient solution had been found – baseball caps given away as free gifts by a tractor company at the *comices agricoles*. The Garry Glitters disappeared, replaced by clones of Bill Clinton.

The crux was the code. In the car I could hear them repeating their numbers like a mantra. The code consisted of four figures only, but those four figures separated richness from poverty. Tubard once got his in the wrong order three times in a row – in itself no mean mathematical feat – and the machine swallowed his card. Upon, which he set about destroying the bank with his head and crash helmet until dissuaded.

Even getting your hands on your money didn't spell the end of the drama. The machine issued a receipt, which could be used to infiltrate their account. What to do with it? Rolling it into a ball and throwing it in a bin was out of the question – the local dustmen would nick them. The solution was supplied by a James Bond

movie broadcast on TF1 in April. They would do what
any spy does with a secret code. Eat it. This explains
why, if you happen to pass by the Crédit Agricole in the
rue Sylvestre-Bonnard in Ligueil at around 12.15 on a
Monday morning, you will come across a gaggle of
baseball-capped *paysans* masticating their receipts.

Once back in the village, we would retire to the
Toison d'Or to celebrate the safe return to civilization
and also to perform a civic gesture. The press had
recently announced the news that the gap between the
amount of wine produced and the amount of wine
drunk in France now totalled some 57 million
hectolitres a year. Huddled together around the bar, we
did our level best to reduce the wine lake.

On this particular day the village was unusually
animated. From afar you could hear the clickety-clack
of the Zimmer frames moving swiftly from house
to house. Shutters were banged open, urgent messages
whispered through letterboxes. The noise of revving
Solexes shattered the morning calm as a flotilla of
orange-crash-helmeted Hell's Angels headed off past
the cemetery in the direction of Mouzay.

'*Viens voir chez Marcellin.*'

'*Nom de Diou nom de Diou nom de Diou!*'

What had Marcellin been up to? Everyone was
heading for the N'Garage.

'*Ça! Il faut le voir.*'

Marcellin had finally done it. But done what? Henri,
his cheeks flushed with rosé and excitement, was quick
to sense the moment.

'*Il y a de la copulation dans l'air.*'

The N mystery I had finally elucidated. Marcellin, for
a long time, had been the local Citroën agent. At first,
relations with the firm were fine and dandy. If he

needed something, all he had to do was to write a letter
and a few weeks later the spare part would arrive on his
doorstep, delivered with a smile and a glass of wine by
le fils Meunier.

Clouds gathered when he had problems with the
sign. Backing a combine harvester into the garage,
Marcellin had dislodged the N of Citroën which fell to
the ground and smashed into tiny pieces. It was impossible to buy a replacement letter. You bought the seven
letters or nothing at all. Marcellin had no desire to buy
and to stock six letters he didn't need, so he refused and
left things as they were. The garage was now called
Citroë. A bad idea. Business dropped off. Tourists
would pass in front of the garage and scratch their
heads. *Citroë? Never heard of it.*

And then a cousin of Penthouse sold Marcellin a tin
of indelible weather-resistant paint. Marcellin got out
his brush and ladder and painted in the missing letter.
The garage was once again called CitroëN and business
got back to normal.

Until computers. Marcellin didn't understand a
thing. A girl came one afternoon to explain and left in
despair. He didn't click at the right time, his fingers
were too wide for the keyboard and he crushed
his mouse. Marcellin was one of the straightforward
generation. If he could, he could, if he couldn't, he
couldn't. He not only decided he couldn't but also that
he wouldn't and threw in his franchise, informing the
firm – by letter – that he was going independent. He
then dismantled the sign, or that part of it which was
dismountable. From that time onwards Marcellin's
garage was called N, with its exotic Afro-Tibetan ring.

Until this morning.

The pavements of Mouzay were unusually busy. At

this time in the morning the only person normally to be seen walking the streets was le Père Fillon looking desperately for the post office which had closed in 1987. Not so today. Today the village was humming. It was difficult to park on the square in front of the church. The white Twingo of the *Nouvelle République* was already in position. A camera crew from FR3 Régions were setting up a satellite dish. A silent crowd had gathered in front of the N'Garage. Parents whispered muted explanations to their children. Photographs were taken. Gendarmes scratched their heads then shook them slowly in compassion.

Marcellin avait craqué. The frustration, the waiting, the fantasizing, the anguish, the jealousy, the wanting, the desire, the loneliness, the mail-order lingerie had finally proved too much. *Il avait dégondé*. He had unhinged himself. In the middle of the night he had gone into the silent garage to find his paint and his brush. He had leaned his ladder against the wall of the garage and, with a torch attached to the top rung, had spent his night painting. Big red letters. Not a splash, not a splodge. *Aucun pâté*. This was the work of a real pro. In the early-morning light he had climbed down to admire his handiwork. He was the Michelangelo of garage signs. The N no longer stood in splendid isolation.

It was now there for all to see – the bigots, the prudes, the freethinkers, the Lefties, the reactionaries, the Masons, the Rotarians, the fraternity of cheesemakers, the brotherhood of tripe. There, big and bold, was Marcellin's masterpiece. Two letters before the N, four after:

M-O-N-I-Q-U-E.

The Tasmalou were dubious. Marcellin had finally dared to declare his love. *Très bien*. Monique Bourdeau, the luscious autumn pear who drove the school bus, could bask in his affections. But there was a downside to Marcellin's outing. Louis, her squat husband, would come back from his North Sea oil rig, read Marcellin's passion written for all to see across the walls of the garage, and trouble would brew.

The weary Marcellin was still asleep. It was decided not to disturb him. This might be his last night of peace. Passion is problematical in the countryside. The market in Ligueil is full of unrequited lovers. The *paysans* in khaki shorts, sandals and socks are not clones of Cedric Pinson. No, sir. They are the lovesick relics of the past, men who lost out and who soothed their wounds with gut rot and Pernod. They had one chance; they let it slip through their fingers. She was promised to another. To the fils Dubarre whose grass was greener, to the fils Champbard whose cows won prizes. Or his father was angry with her father. Or his grandfather with her grandfather. Or his great-grandfather with her great-grandfather. She didn't want to but she had to obey. And happiness passed them by, like a school bus which refused to stop. The candle was doused, a long gone flame in the wind.

In the evening, in the dusk at the bottom of the garden, I poured out my soul to the leeks. I had no intention of ending up like the lovers of Ligueil. Sandals, socks and shorts were not my cup of tea.

All ideas of spelling out L-O-U in leeks were shelved.

20

What fun. It was Gérard's birthday.

I had always thought my rival looked pretty old – a little on the jaded and jilted side – but Lou assured me he was in fact quite young. Odd. Perhaps opticians wear out faster than common mortals.

Gérard was a Gemini: distinctive astrological signs, if my memory served me right; cunning, hairy, with bad breath and greasy.

His friends were giving him a party. Lou asked me along. She very much wanted us to be buddies. For the time being we were even. He'd pulled a fast one with his tropical catalogue, I'd massacred his goose. Lou, sensing – enjoying? – our rivalry, sought to reconcile us. In the car she painted a flattering portrait of her one-time lover – a sensitive chap with a heart of gold who found it very difficult to live with so much money. Poor little thing. My heart bled for him.

'If he's so wonderful, why leave him?' I asked sulkily.

Lou immersed me in the acid of her gaze. If I were to continue to ask such stupid questions, she warned me, she might think of changing her mind.

And what did darling Gérard think of me? His impression was that I was arrogant, scornful, cold, clever and not against brutalizing dead poultry. Some people read the dregs in coffee cups. Gérard obviously read snot in swimming pools. How else could he get me so wrong?

The bash was to take place in the country house of Bob, an old schoolfriend of Gérard's, now the Managing Director of a factory in Saumur which made hinges. I parked the Mazda in a car park – the direction was announced by arrow-shaped signposts in the lawn – surrounded by huge four-wheel drives with their tinted windows and anti-bison bumpers. Could they be preparing an invasion of Pincé le Petit, the village up the road?

The house was ugly and overweight, a large thing with no particular shape, too vulgar to be old, too pretentious to be attractive. On the terrace were a collection of rustic wheelbarrows full of fluorescent geraniums, alongside a statue of a nymph which doubtless came from Castorama and which Auguste Renard could have used to decorate his bin. Inside, the terracotta floor tiles had been laid in a diamond pattern. In the entrance a juke box, on the right a billiard table. Faded landscapes of sad countrysides in heavy frames were hung too high on the walls with their *fleur de lys* wallpaper. A bar had been built out of old beams and bricks. A series of low leather sofas gathered around a plasma screen like a herd of deflated cows. On the coffee-table stood an ice-bucket in the form of a top hat. From downstairs came the noise of an exciting table-tennis match. A large hi-fi machine with its huge amplifier and leads hidden behind a row of leather-bound Reader's Digest Books of the Year was playing *un best of* the hits of the plump middle-aged pop singer Eddy Mitchell.

The guests were gathered around the Habitat barbecue on wheels. They all broke out into mock exasperation as we arrived.

'*Ah!*'

'*Enfin!*'

'*Quand même!*' I mean to say . . .

But the chipolatas were still in their vacuum packs. All this talk of time was meaningless badinage. Bob, the host, was the Honorary President of the Saumur Armoured Tank Museum. He was proud to show us a snap of their newest acquisition: a large Sherman complete with original caterpillar tracks. We were all suitably impressed. What a lovely tank! What a snip! Antoine, his white opened-neck shirt revealing a gold chain embossed with his name, was the owner of a local nursery, Bertrand ran a sawmill, Gilles a chain of sports shops. They all expressed their admiration and support for the Medef which I took to be some North African dignitary – Sidi Medef? – but which turned out to be the acronym for the French CBI.

Their wives were of the interchangeable kind, each looking and sounding very much like the next. They were called Babette, Blandine and Marilou and were pert, pretty, brown and lifted. They wore tight-waisted suede trousers, silk shirts and the occasional blazer. They'd just come back from Egypt and would soon be leaving for Thailand. They adored both their personal trainer – *il est chou* – and their golf professional – *il est très chou*.

Conversation was overdone, their level of enthusiasm too high. A disparity transpired between the subject in hand – shoes, a new talkshow – and the commentary it engendered. They would say:

'*Non! Incroyable! Epouvantable! Génial!*' when they should have said: '*Bof. Pas mal. Nul.*'

Gérard had been ill-advised to wear a baseball cap which accentuated his optician's profile. I asked myself

the following existential question: how the hell could
Lou have ever gone out with a man who wore a baseball cap? Fortunately I stopped, chiding myself. I was
ashamed of my prejudice. A person is free to wear
what he or she wants. If Gérard desired to look like a
demented Texan, it was his right to do so.

They were all delighted to see Lou – '*Ça fait vraiment
longtemps*' – and proved masters in the art of the
compliment:

'*Bella . . .*'

'*Tu es en pleine forme.*'

'*Ah! Ses yeux verts . . .*'

'*Pas mal, la nana!*'

They touched her, caressed her and kneaded her as if
she belonged to them. I looked around for a fly swat to
keep them at distance, but the barbecue was swatless.

While the enemy were doing their utmost to eliminate
me, I served myself a slug of rosé – a tart *assemblage*
of young rhubarb and owl's piss, marketed under the
VDQS – Very Dangerous/Quality Suspicious – label, by
a conglomerate of wine-growers who, unable to sell to
their one-time clientèle, had decided to wreak revenge
and to dissolve them in acid.

The kitchen was a hive of activity although there was
nothing to be done because we were going to grill a
large beef rib. In order to ingratiate myself with the
reluctant company I explained that in Oxford, to cook
a steak, we would slip it in the toaster. Ha-ha. That
we ironed kippers to warm them up. Ha-ha. I was on
the point of slipping sardines down their trousers to
illustrate a novel way of preparing oily fish but decided
against it.

The beef was served *bleu* – the chic way, which
means cold and flaccid. I slipped a slice in the toaster.

The sauté potatoes were half-burned, half-uncooked. A sauté potato requires love and attention, but the present company were too intent on scuppering me and giving Lou back to Gérard as a birthday present.

What they most appreciated about the English, they said, was that we apparently kept women in their place. Beef seemed to tickle their misogyny. Shamefaced, but to keep my end up, I told a joke. I had to start three times because they kept interrupting.

'Non, Gilles!'

'Chut!'

'Laisse-le raconter!'

A couple had been married for years. One day the wife died. As she was being carried into the church for the funeral, one of the pallbearers slipped, banged the coffin against the wall. There was a sudden stirring from inside the box. A miracle! She was still alive. She was taken out of the coffin and husband and wife spent another ten years together. At the end of which time, the wife died again. The funeral was rearranged but this time, as the pallbearers carried the coffin into the church, the husband whispered urgently, 'Mind the wall!'

There was no question of laughing at my joke. That would be fraternizing with the enemy. The awkward silence was interrupted by the arrival of the birthday cake. They asked me what the plural of un petit beurre was. Des petits beurres? No. They all fell about. Ils sont cons, ces rosbifs! The plural of un petit beurre is des touyous. I didn't understand. They laughed until they cried. Didn't I know the song?

'Un petit beurre, des touyous.'

It took me ten minutes to get the phonetics worked out. ''Appy birthday to you'. Hilarious.

Gérard was showered with presents he didn't need because he already owned everything. We gave him a *moules marinières* shower gel.

The afternoon had been set aside for the confrontation. I had to be pitted against Gérard and lose. The Viking marauders from the north must be punished for pillaging and raping the beauties of the Loire Valley. What could they suggest? Tennis? I imagined myself on the other side of the net as Gérard spent the afternoon aiming cannon balls at my undercarriage.

'*Désolé*. Bad elbow'.

A swimming race? No question of slipping into my pink Bermudas in front of these lithe executives with their rippling torsos. A lifetime of dumplings and fish and chips had left its mark. I declined.

'*Un petit rhume,*' I coughed delicately.

The surfboard? You'd never catch a gentleman frolicking on a piece of polystyrene. Hot-air ballooning? Vertigo. Bridge? Never played. They began to look desperate. How the hell were they going to make me look ridiculous? How could they prove to Lou Charpin that she had made the wrong choice? Then someone came up with a bright idea and I surrendered.

On arriving, I had spotted the minigolf course on the lawn behind the house. Each green was decorated with a chipboard replica of one of the Châteaux de la Loire. Little did they know that in Abesbury – without in any way being tigerwoodish – I had quite a reputation. If I were to defend the honour of my country, let clock golf be the weapon of choice.

Everyone was excited. Gérard started to do press-ups. His advisors huddled around him. I thought about suggesting roping Lou to a pole in view of the ninth hole – the winner taking the damsel as a trophy – but this was putting (if you'll excuse the pun) too much at risk. As it turned out, we were very well-matched. Until hole five – the Château de Chambord – we were neck and neck. The golf was concentrated and impressive. It was for the last four holes – from Cheverny on – that cheating became essential.

There are two ways of cheating: the French way and the English way. The English tend to cheat openly. We trip over the ball, knock it sideways, apologize profusely and puts it back where it hadn't been before.

'Terribly sorry.'

The French version is at once more straightforward and more devious.

'*Eh dis-donc,*' said Gérard, pointing up at the sky and drawing our attention to the Paris-Madrid passing overhead as he gave his ball a gentle knock in the right direction. And so we continued, I ever more clumsy and Gérard ever more keen on plane-spotting. The much vaunted 'fairplay' amounts to nothing more than this: accepting with grace and good humour each other's skulduggery.

His ball disappeared in the moat of Azay le Rideau, mine knocked over a turret of Ussé, we both lodged ourselves in the gates of Blois and arrived, bloody but unbowed, before the arches of the Castle of Chenonceaux with twenty-three points each. A real cliffhanger. The spectators were quiet. This was a solemn moment.

Gérard was the first to play. He took position. Several times mimed the stroke. Stopped, wiped his hands on a Kleenex, discussed with his advisors the arabesque his club was to describe, took position once again, shot and the ball gently, decidedly, determinedly passed through the arches of the bridge. Bravo, Gérard! He threw himself into their arms. They kissed and hugged.

The moment was filmed in order to be played back in slow motion for future generations.

The game was not yet over, of course. I had still to play. I went through the same preparatory rigmarole, although no one seemed to be interested in discussing my arabesques. Too bad. I took aim and played. The ball, like a mini white cannon ball, began to head straight as a die towards the hole. We held our breath. And as we did so I played my masterstroke.

One final devious gesture was essential. At the very last moment, just as the ball was to pass unscathed under the bridge, I pretended to flick a petal out of the way of its trajectory and at the same time gave it the gentlest of knocks with my finger. This slight inflection of the flight path produced the desired result. Bang. The ball knocked into the arch of the bridge and bounced back. Gérard had won.

The explosion of joy behind me was very moving. Gérard, the Birthday Boy in person, was pummelled and carried shoulder-high from the clock golf-course.

'On a gagné!'

'Les doigts dans le nez!'

'Il a perdu . . .'*

And then, inevitably, 'Allez, les Bleus!'

I stood on one side, remaining tactfully and respectfully remote from the rejoicing. As I cleaned the clubs and was putting them back in the bag on wheels, Lou joined me.

'Mike,' she was tender. 'You lose so well.' And she comforted me, giving me a hug, stroking my hair.

Behind me, the rejoicing abruptly stopped. What

---

* This ritual ends *le doigt dans le cul* but the final line, for the sake of politeness, is often omitted.

the hell was going on? Why wasn't Lou Charpin congratulating mighty Gérard the *rosbif* crusher?

I looked at them with compassion. They had things to learn. Poor fools. Winning? It's easy to win. Almost vulgar. Anyone can win. But losing . . . and losing with style – that's an achievement. That takes real class.

The cries of victory died down. Lou slipped her arm in mine. I waved in their direction.

'*Bravo, Gérard. Génial. Bravo!*'

It was his turn to go pale.

Perfide Albion?

Who – us?

21

In the weeks leading up to the summer holidays, the British tabloids are full of stories of the appalling habits of our continental neighbours. Before leaving for the packed beaches of the Mediterranean, the French throw their pets down the loo. Farewell hamsters, gerbils, and goldfish. Care must be taken during August. When you open the tap, a pet may pop out.

Mathilde, one of the three daughters of Cécile the doormat and Thierry the Porsche, was leaving for the coast with her parents. The immediate problem was Vanessa, her pet rabbit. There was no question, declared Thierry, of disturbing the peace of his well-earned sojourn. He could already see landlords scrutinizing fitted carpets looking for telltale turds.

What was to be done with the aforesaid bunny? No question either of asking Dylan. He was preparing for his *Baccalauréat* – and his scene was canaries. Lou would be correcting the *Baccalauréat*. Rémi disapproved of bourgeois sentimentality. Laurent was busy with Bulgaria, Sylvie was allergic. Only one candidate remained. He lived in the country, smiled all the time and, suffering from acute sycophancia, had never been known to refuse anything.

Not even Vanessa.

Whom Thierry left with me on the Friday before their Saturday-morning departure.

'*Elle pue*. She stinks!' he complained loudly. 'I nearly died in the car. *Chie sans arrêt*. Never stops shitting.' He gave me some pills. 'Shove these in her food. *Sinon, essaie un bouchon*. Try a cork.'

Wink. 'Nubiddy's perfact.'

He walked around the farmhouse knocking bits of plaster from the wall and scraping the woodwork with his finger.

'*Et n'oublie pas*', he added. 'Don't forget. Be in at six every evening.'

Why?

'*Pour Mathilde. Pour répondre.*'

Of course. Every day Mathilde rings her rabbit. *Pas de problème*. Or *pas de lézard*, although this hardly seemed apposite in the case of rabbits.

Vanessa and I remained alone in the silence of the house looking quizzically at each other. She was of average build, beige-ish and generally quivery. I sang her a few bars of 'All Shook Up' but she was not amused. Her long ears moved like antennae and her nose was extremely mobile. The same could not be said of her dazed, expressionless eyes. In her cage was a trapeze – of the kind that Vanessa Paradis swings on in the perfume ad. I tried to put her on it but she fell off.

Her food was disgusting – evil-smelling pellets made of droppings and pigeon's piss kept in a jam-jar. She didn't seem too keen either. As an apéritif she did however consume the lingerie pages of the La Redoute mail order catalogue.

At six p.m., as promised, on the dot came *DDDrrrriiiinnnggg* – the special noise French phones make. I took Vanessa out of her cage which accelerated the trembling. It was like trying to keep hold of a furry jelly. I took her to the phone and put the receiver to her

ear. She couldn't give a fart. I reassured Mathilde that
Vanessa was having a whale of a time, all the while
trying to hold Houdini in my arms.

Vanessa had to calm down. She must feel at ease
with me. She must feel at home. She must not want to
leave when her mistress returned. This would stand
me in good stead with the family on the animal-loving
front.

I decided to keep a diary.

DAY ONE:

My intention was to build a relationship with
the rabbit. Her natural reticence led me to approach
the challenge with circumspection. This morning I rose
early and placed the cage outside in the glistening
dew of the dawn lawn. I then opened the door – a kind
of blue plastic portcullis – and hid behind a bush to
observe.

Vanessa was sensitive to this gesture of trust. The
nasal quivering was more intermittent and her once
glazed eyes were invaded by an expression of curiosity
and gratitude. The vista before her awakened long-
buried atavistic memories of the primeval pre-pet era
when rabbits were predators in the jungle of life.

After a long hesitation Vanessa ventured outside.
Our beating hearts were doubtless in unison. She
smelled the heady call of freedom, nibbled a leaf and
went back inside. I understood. Too much too soon
could be dangerous for such a delicate metabolism. But
in the evening, when I carried the cage back into the
house our eyes met and Vanessa blinked. No, not
blinked. Winked. Vanessa winked at me. This rabbit
wink brought warmth to my heart. It also encouraged
my endeavour.

On the phone with Mathilde I was tender.

Tomorrow, I said, Vanessa and I would attempt a little walk together.

DAY TWO:

The bitch. She's done a bunk.

I was naïve, sentimental, trusting. I thought that I'd begun to twig what makes rabbits tick. That I would soon pierce the mystery of her quivering, that she would calm down, come when I whistled, smile at my jokes.

Fool that I was. As soon as my back was turned, she pissed off.

Never trust a rabbit.

At first, I thought this was just a little game. I went around the house on all fours pretending to be having fun. 'I know you're hiding, Vanessa, you naughty girl. Come on. Game's up. Where are you?' But no. That wasn't her under the bed, that was a ball of fluff. That wasn't her at the back of the cupboard, that was a scrap of old carpet. Finally I decided to resort to violence. I plugged in the hair-drier and switched it on. If she wouldn't come out of hiding I'd blow her out, and burn her pretty little arse in the process.

Ddddrrriiinnnggg!

Merde! I'd forgotten the 6 p.m. phone call.

'*Bonsoir, Mathilde.*'

'*Elle va bien, Vanessa?*'

And there I was, standing at the phone, a grown man, Oxford-educated, civilized, charming, reduced to imitating an absent rabbit in order to keep my love alive. I showed my teeth, I scratched my pullover, I quivered, I even managed to get my nose to move, I purred.

Do rabbits purr?

DAY THREE:

The neighbours were not over-impressed by my

plight. Aimé Matou was patently sardonic. Three cows perhaps, a wife maybe, but all this fuss for a rabbit? He scratched his head in bewilderment. What with foxes and myxomtosis, Vanessa's chances of survival were nil. He grinned.

'On l'aura bouffée, votre lapine!' Your rabbit will have been eaten by now.

I nailed a notice to the fence at the bottom of the cherry-tree drive: *Warning, rabbit at large* and sello-taped a sticker to the rear window of the Mazda: *Lost, a rabbit answering if in a good mood to the name Vanessa. Distinctive features: big ears, white tail, predilection for mail order catalogues.* Balzac would have done a shade better. I left a copy at the Town Hall.

At six o'clock I once again imitated a rabbit. At least I was getting better at it. The cage I left all night in the courtyard with the door open in case a sudden rush of commonsense reached her nostrils and she yearned for security. Nothing doing. She was doubtless bopping away in a nightclub with a rabbit optician. *La salope.* The slut!

DAY FOUR:

I didn't catch a rabbit. I caught a hedgehog. The little devil had got into the cage and rolled himself into a prickly ball. It is incredibly difficult to dislodge a surly hedgehog from a rabbit's cage. In the end I had to use a spaghetti spoon. The little sod farted in my face. I began to find nature repugnant.

The *gendarmes* found me totally loony when I phoned them.

'You've lost a *what, monsieur?*'

'*Une lapine.*' Silence at the other end.

Then: '*Votre nom, Monsieur?*'

'Monsieur Sadler.'

Sadler. An Englishman. *Tout s'explique*. Last summer they had to issue a search warrant for an errant budgie. *Ces Anglais quand même*.

Ddddrrrriiiinngggg. The evening torture.

'*Qu'est-ce qu'elle a fait aujourd'hui, Vanessa?*'

Today? Today, Vanessa was a very naughty rabbit.

DAY FIVE:

Bumped into Tubard on the way to a Tasmalou orgy. He, at least, was sympathetic. I admired his *quatre quarts* with *gnôle*-soaked sultanas which made it the world's most lethal fruitcake. He advised me to consult Père Jules who ran a rabbit farm. All I had to do was to buy a lookalike – *un sosie*. What difference is there between one rabbit and the next?

Une idée lumineuse. I'd get on to it straight away.

I knocked at the door, which was opened after a certain amount of banging from within – the knocking over of stuffed badgers from the sideboard – by Père Jules in person, complete with his headgear, his eternally askew orange crash helmet which he wore to bed. He was just back from his garden and in a bad mood.

'*Les salauds,*' he grunted and, miming a shotgun, decimated the enemy whose heads were popping out of the lino. *Pan pan* went the French shotgun. And the enemy – an army of imaginary moles – fell lifeless to the floor. *Pan pan*. The transistors he had wired to his fruit trees kept the birds at bay but moles were deaf. With the result that they had dug galleries deep into his vegetable garden. But Père Jules was not to be beaten. His one visible eye twinkled under the visor of the crash helmet.

'*Elles vont voir ce qu'elles vont voir.*'

He then mimed screwing a rubber tube to the

exhaust pipe of his Solex moped. The other end of the tube he pushed down the mole-holes which sprang up all over his salon. There was one under the 1985 Thomson telly, another under the *buffet*. He then revved up the engine, and pulled back the throttle.

'*Vrrrraaaaaoooouuuuummmm. Vrrrraaaaaoooouuuu-ummmm.*'

There ensued a moving dumbshow. Père Jules became a mole reading his *Nouvelle République* in the front room of his mole-hole. The mole put down his local paper, sniffed the air, started to cough and then panicked, gasping for fresh air, scratching and scrabbling as he frantically climbed the gallery shaft and popped out . . . only to come eye to eye with Père Jules in person, waiting to blow his brains out.

'*PAN. PAN.*'

A mole exploded under the table. Another under the armchair. *Pan pan.* Soon the room was full of imaginary dead moles. It was *Wind in the Willows* directed by Quentin Tarentino.

Eventually, Père Jules calmed down and, ready for conversation, took a bottle of *gnôle* from the cupboard under the kitchen sink where it was also used, when not in the apéritif mode, for paint-stripping and drain-clearing. I panicked. Desirous of protecting throat and tonsils I rapidly blurted out the reasons for my visit.

'*Une lapine, Père Jules! J'ai besoin d'une lapine!*'

My kingdom for a rabbit.

Père Jules put down the bottle and went outside. I followed him into the garden and found myself in a rabbit supermarket, a nirvana of bunnies. Brown ones, white ones, grey ones, russet ones, spotted ones. Little tails wagging as far as the eye could see. I started my inspection. One of them had a *je ne sais quoi* of

Ségolène Royal and a toothy one reminded me of Jane Birkin. But Vanessa . . .? I ended up by selecting a cute little thing with a turned-up nose.

'*C'est combien?*' I asked.

Père Jules wrote *5 Euros* down on his paper pad all the while looking over his shoulder in case the taxman was spying on him with binoculars from the upstairs window of the Toison d'Or. I only had a 50 Euro note. He went out to get change. He seemed to be gone a long time. I had time to read all the articles in the *Télé 7 Jours* dated April 1996. Finally he returned. With my rabbit.

'*Voilà!*'

In a plastic bag. Skinned. Plucked. Gutted. Oven ready.

Bon.

So much for the lookalike. I was at my lowest ebb. There was nothing for it. I pushed my glass forward.

'I believe you had suggested a quick *gnôle*, Père Jules?'

I returned home.

Drrrriiinnngg!

'Today Mathilde, it was very hot. And do you know what Vanessa did? She took her coat off.'

DAY SIX:

Very depressed.

Disconsolate, I wandered around the garden. I had to face up to the fact. Vanessa had done a permanent bunk. I had been seduced and abandoned. It was a classic case. I was the rabbit Ariadne, left to pine on my rock.

Squelch. What . . . *Tiens! Une crotte*. I had trodden in a small fresh turd . . . and another. There was a whole rosary of *crottes* on the drive. Strange. Suddenly there was a crackling and shuffling in the hornbeam edge. A branch shook, a leaf moved. Just a minute . . .

There she was, staring out at me from the undergrowth. Smiling coyly, showing her teeth, twitching her button nose. And in her eyes a look of compassion, as if asking forgiveness. The Prodigal Rabbit was home.

There is a famous moment in *La Femme du Boulanger* by Marcel Pagnol when Raimu the actor, instead of scolding his errant wife, turns his anger on Pomponette, his cat, who has just returned from a night on the tiles.

'*Regarde, la voilà la Pomponette! Garce, salope, ordure . . . C'est maintenant que tu reviens?*'

I knew how the baker felt. Vanessa must have spent two days in the toolshed living off electric cable and putty. But I was so happy to see her back home that I refrained from scolding. I took her in my arms, gave her a cuddle and tweaked her nose.

Vanessa taught me a lesson. There's no point hesitating. Nothing to be gained from leaving the door open.

It was time for action.

22

Enfin. D Day. *Le Jour J.*

The party spirit had invaded Loches. Huge billboards concealed the majestic Renaissance façade of the *mairie*, proclaiming to the world the highlight of the cultural season: *Festival lyrique. Le Parc Baschet: Rossini's* William Tell *by the Orchestra and Chorus of the Lyrica Bulgarica: maestro Boris Bolchkov.*

Local confectioners had invented a cake to celebrate the occasion. *Le Guillaume* – the William Tell – was a light, nutty sponge, with a coffee-cream filling and Chantilly cream icing. In order to distinguish it from the *Agnès* – named after the local Renaissance celebrity Agnès Sorel, world famous for a portrait showing her with one naked breast (the cake was a coconut milk blancmange topped by a red cherry), the *pâtissiers* had come up with a novel idea. To ward off boredom, patients in the local psychiatric ward had spent their afternoons making cardboard arrows. Thus, a stylish hand-painted arrow pierced each and every cake.

The idea was quick to catch on. Elegant ladies wore arrows through their hats. Assistants in the Crédit Agricole arranged loans with arrows through their heads. Mortier Optical was one of the sponsors. His logo? A pair of spectacles with an arrow through one lens. The whole town was in the grip of *la Tell attitude*.

Music was everywhere. To the annoyance of the

population, the *Union Commercial* had concealed
loudspeakers in every tree, ledge, nook and cranny.
From ten in the morning to closing time, the system
blared out non-stop Rossini overtures. The music did
not produce the desired effect, however. The lively
rhythms were such that the Lochois, normally given to
strolling, did their shopping in record time – much to
the despair of the aforesaid *Union Commercial*. The
Rossini was soon replaced by the usual French tape
of American standards sung in unrecognizable English
by elderly pop stars, and shopping returned to its
normal pace.

The arrival of the musicians – portly Bulgarian
singers in outmoded dark suits and young string-players
in microskirts – brought a new lease of life to the town.
Laurent immediately abandoned his business activities
to give himself over to *l'art lyrique*.

The town became one big stage set. The guests sang
as they shopped, sang as they supped. Deep resonant
bass voices were to be heard on every street corner,
giving pacemakers palpitations and causing a truckle
of *vieux cantal* to split into two on a market cheese-
stall. The maestro Bolchkov was the toast of the town.
As round and as appetizing as the fruit which starred in
the opera, he only knew one word of French – *rillettes* –
which he put to good use, consuming endless pots of
the pork paté using his finger as a spoon. *Rrrr-illettes!*

On the eve of the première, an official reception was
held at the *mairie*. In a large echoing room with –
surprisingly – tartan wallpaper, eight dignitaries made
exactly the same long speech, congratulating the same
organizers and thanking the same organizations using
precisely the same adjectives. This is a tradition in
France. If you happen to nod off during one speech,

you can always catch up on the next. You can also make bets. Who'd be the shortest? This evening the Conseil Régional beat the Conseil Général by 23 seconds. *Bravo la Région*!

Laurent had called on the family to lend a helping hand. I mucked in, serving *amuse-gueules* on a silver tray. When I went out into the corridor to replenish my tray of Super-U green olive tapenade, I bumped into my brother-in-law in the arms of a voluptuous Bulgarian violinist busy rolling a shovel. He broke off. I presumed he was going to ask for a hand attaching her to the radiators, but no. He sought understanding.

'*C'est elle – ma reine*, Anna Pavlovna. It was to her I was talking on the phone in the garden. I know that you speak Bulgarian. You said nothing to Gisèle. I can trust you. *Tu es mon frère*.'

And he returned to the highly strung instrument in his arms. *Tuer le cochon?* Laurent had never been tempted.

His trust was built on my deceit. I felt embarrassed when, on the morning of the concert, I bumped into Gisèle. She was in tears. Had she finally understood the key to her fickle husband's melomania? *Malheureusement pas*. It was Dylan who was the problem. Returning home unexpectedly, she came across her son on all fours in the garden, pissing himself with laughter. Had Dylan gone nuts? Her concern intensified when she saw that he was sowing his canary seed in the flowerbed. She was on the point of ringing the psychiatry unit when Dylan, red-eyed and not quite in possession of himself, spilled the beans. He couldn't give a fart about canaries or Vermeer, he told her. Why did he go to Holland to buy his birdseed? Because Dutch birdseed contains cannabis. *Du shit, maman!* He found this hilarious. He'd taken them all for a ride. Before, he'd grown the weed in the windowboxes *chez Edouard*. Now he could have it homegrown.

Gisèle est tombée des nues. She fell out of the clouds. There, on all fours in the garden in front of her, was her son, *son chéri*, the future Director of the Louvre Museum, revealed to be no more than a bucolic junky.

Tears poured down her face. Laurent must not be told. Not now. Not yet. He had enough on his plate. Poor Laurent. Gisèle's hands wrung her lace handkerchief. If you only saw the state he was in! Since the arrival of the Bulgarians she had hardly seen him. She was convinced he wasn't getting enough sleep. For once she was right.

Lou arrived mid-morning from a *Baccalauréat* examiners' meeting in Orléans. She was in a bad mood. Her colleagues were petty and small-minded. She was once again going to chuck it all in and open a flower shop. A giant *paëlla* was to be served to cast and guests at the end of the performance. When the unfortunate cook was discovered decorating the tables with plastic flowers, the grammarian erupted.

'*C'est quoi, cette merde?*' she stormed.

She wanted real flowers. She wanted wild flowers. Teams were sent out into the fields to calm her down as we administered tea, a poppy, and an organic croissant. This evening I was going to propose. If she was in a state, it would be like diving into a volcano.

Our immediate concern was with the weather. As this was an open-air performance, our fate was in the lap of the gods. It would be impossible to perform *William Tell* in the rain, since the arrows would go soft. Père Simon, a wizened old man of 133 with four teeth and a Gauloise stuck between them, forecast a raincloud heading south-east in our direction. Planes took off from the military air base at Parçay-Meslay to intercept and to destroy the airborne iceberg.

It did rain early afternoon – just a few drops, but sufficient to cause the ink to run on the notices which had been sellotaped to the chairs in the front two rows. The seats had to be scrubbed down and dried. There was no question of having the visitors walking around with the word RESERVED stamped on their bums.

Cocktails were served from six o'clock in the handsome townhouse of the Cultural Attaché. Lou was reluctant to rub shoulders with Ariane Tricot whom she suspected of having participated in the earlier chapters of my continental education. On arriving at the house I gave myself away by brushing aside the Virginia creeper in order to find the bellrope and thereby avoid a shower of pigeon shit. Lou was sardonic.

'I see that Monsieur knows his way around . . .'

Well, she still had the key to the Palais Mortier. It was *kif kif*. Fifty fifty. But this was no time to argue. The door opened and Ariane, her lithe brown arms emerging temptingly from a white sleeveless silk vest, greeted me with enthusiasm.

'*Maï-quel! Quel plaisir.*'

She then sent a brittle smile in the direction of Lou. They eyed each other, shank, pastern, fetlock. I endeavoured to break the ice.

'You have, I believe, already met. At the fancy-dress party, at Pont de Ruan.'

'Ah,' said Ariane, adding acid to her voice, 'so it was you who was locked inside . . .'

'And so it was you who was locked outside . . .'

Fortunately Brice, Monsieur Tricot, resplendent in a kilt made out of the Town Hall wallpaper, turned up

to serve a Cabernet Sauvignon which, given its colour
and lack of body, was doubtless Norwegian. As Lou
inspected the house, Ariane took me to one side in
the kitchen.

'*Alors, Maï-quel* . . .'

'Yes, Ariane?'

'*Mon petit Anglais est amoureux?*'

I refused to reply, being neither hers nor small.

'*Une française, c'est si compliqué* . . . *N'est-ce pas,
Maï-quel?*' And she moved in closer as if to add a dash
of complication. '*Et tu lui as parlé de nos peccadilles?*'

No, as it happened, I hadn't gone into the details of
our peccadilloes.

'*Tu lui as parlé de nos pelles et de nos patins?*'

I could safely say that all conversations with Lou had
until now been shovel free and skateless. The kitchen
door opened. Lou eyed us with sharp suspicion which
Ariane was quick to encourage.

'Maï-quel was once *mon professeur d'anglais.*
"Once" – eez zat correct, Maï-quel? We were just
revising. *N'est-ce pas, Maï-quel?*'

Before Lou could tackle her from behind, an ebullient
beaming Italian loomed from nowhere, oozing *bellos*
and *bellas* and squeezing everyone's cheek. This was
Ariane's new teacher. I recognized her strategy. The
children didn't have time for lessons and Ariane had
gallantly stepped into the breech. Aldo was black-
haired, unshaven and charming, with an open-neck
white shirt revealing a gold chain depicting Cupid firing
an arrow. I had parked the Mazda next to his gondola
on the *mail*. We all had a great time saying: '*Va bene*',
which eased the danger of any international incident.

Lou had by now completed her inspection of the
house, judging the decoration to be tight-arsed and

constipated, what with its flowery poufs (the ex-women in my life seemed to have a predilection for poufs) and tasselled lampshades (*idem*). She wanted to get the hell out of the place. As we were leaving, I espied Gisèle drowning her sorrows in a lonely corner. I slipped her a bottle of Brice's oldest single malt, which he kept hidden in the bookcase. She put her finger to her lips. *Motus et bouche cousue*.

The show was due to begin at nine o'clock. Lou left to find Rémi, who was leading a delegation from St Pierre des Corps to meet with the Weight Watchers from the ex-Soviet bloc. Mortier was in the vicinity. I'd seen his tank in the sponsors' car park under the walls of the old town. A quick kick in the tyres had delighted a gang of local stray dogs who, hoping to set the alarm off again, had proceeded to piss all over it. Thierry arrived with the girls and the rabbit.

'*Elle aime beaucoup l'opéra, Vanessa?*' I enquired.

Cécile followed 100 metres behind, staggering under the load of the picnic-basket, the travelling rugs and the medicine chest – in the event of an attack by malevolent mosquitoes. The children had gone to private lessons to study the libretto, which Hortense began to recite to me as Vanessa shat on my shoes:

'It's the story of the famous Swiss patriot William Tell who foments a revolt against the tyrant Gessler. One morning . . .'

The Bulgarian trumpets sounded the beginning of the performance. We all sat down, taking great care to wipe the Formica seat beforehand. Nothing like a wet arse to come between the *aficionado* and his passion.

The natural setting of the Parc Baschet was pure magic. The backdrop of the crumbling, pock-marked limestone walls of the dungeon, the distant spires of

Saint-Ours, the lush evening Touraine landscape at our feet – pure romance. I looked around me. Lou must have remained with Rémi. I was sure that I had chosen the right place and the right time. It was now simply a question of putting the plan into operation.

The Maestro Bolchkov appeared to the applause of audience and orchestra. He was wearing tails that were several sizes too small and which emitted an odour of Bulgarian mothballs. He acknowledged the polite ovation, bowed, busting a button on his waist-band, turned to face his orchestra of bank clerks and bimbos, raised his baton and . . . we were off.

Rossini was quick to enchant. Even the bats put their little heads out of their niches in the wall to sing along in the big numbers. All went well until Boris was attacked by a mosquito. He attempted to ward it off by lashing out, d'Artagnan-like, with his baton. The orchestra followed suit and Rossini accelerated frenetically until the mosquito, doubtless suffocated by the mothball aroma, dropped dead and the opera resumed its normal pace. Anna Pavlovna was sitting in the front row of musicians in the shadow of Boris. Her concentration was a delight to behold. Totally enraptured by the music, the rhythmic movements of her bow caused her short skirt to ride so far up her thighs that she was in danger of giving us a peek at her Christmas present. *Quelle soirée.*

The interval came after the arson of the thatched cottages, perpetrated by the villainous Gessler and just as the rebels begin to foment their sedition. The suspense was at its height. Night had fallen and, after having watched a couple of hours of brightly lit opera, no one could see anything and we all kept falling over, which added extra fun to an already exciting evening.

The audience staggered about blindly in the dark heading for one of the makeshift bars – wooden Swiss huts containing a plastic bath of ice to keep the Vouvray cool. After two uninterrupted hours of Bulgarian lyricism, getting plastered seemed only sensible.

Lou was debating with the *paëlla*-maker. The Spanish supper was to be served immediately at the end of the Swiss opera. When exactly was he to light the fire under his pans? Leaving them in heated discussion, I retired to put the finishing touches to my amorous *mise en scène*.

The décor I had chosen was an abandoned turret giving on to the moonlit River Indre which flowed at its foot. The medieval ruin was invaded by creeper – I am not referring to myself – and the old worn stone made the setting look as if it was an illustration from a Walter Scott novel. I'd not read Walter Scott and trusted that the associations were none too haggis-y. The place did smell a bit dank but, ever thoughtful, I had brought along my *Nights of Seville* room deodorant spray, last used on the hedgehog in Vanessa's cage. I gave the turret a thorough squirting, the whole place suddenly smelling like a marmalade factory. It was essential that all go according to plan. At the end of the opera, as she was still in the thrall of the music, I would whisk Lou away to my sweet-smelling castle and pop the question.

'*Accepterais-tu de prendre le rosbif ici présent pour époux?*'

This is what I was going to say. I had planned the sentence. Not too poker-faced, a shade quirky, but grammatically correct. Marcellin had screwed up his declaration. I didn't intend to make the same balls-up.

The trumpets sounded and we staggered back to our places where the seditious choir awaited us, ready to break into full-throated revolt. The second part of the evening somewhat lacked the discipline of the first. The *Préfet* fell asleep on the shoulder of the Mayor who, being of the same political leaning, didn't dare wake him up. The critic from the *Renaissance Lochoise* newspaper began to snore, which was a cue for half of the audience to follow suit. At the beginning of the Fifth Act a squadron of bats was released from the wall to fly low over everyone's heads to wake them up in time for the curtain calls. The disaster, however, came with the finale and the *paëlla*. Lou and the cook had perfected their timing. Twelve pages before the end, he would begin to reheat his vast pans of prawns and gambas.

The light breeze was quick to waft whiffs of Andalusian seafood under the noses of the Bulgarian artists. The effect was immediate. The orchestra lost control. The singers started to salivate, the strings to dribble and Boris to have hallucinations. His baton was transformed by his gastronomic imagination into a huge brochette on which were impaled glistening grilled shellfish. It was clear for all to hear. The Lyrica Bulgarica had travelled thousands of miles across Europe in a bus with bad brakes and dodgy tyres driven by the deep-seated desire to tuck into a municipal *paëlla*.

The music came to an end with the death of the tyrant, was widely applauded, and a rousing hymn was sung in honour of Swiss patriotism. The bravos and the bows were heartfelt but perfunctory. The stampede towards the tables had already begun – the orchestra leading the way, and a hungry Boris trampling his groupies underfoot.

'*Rrrrr-illettes! Rrrrr-illettes!*'

I pushed and shoved my way through the chorus

of Swiss villagers stuffing saffron down their throats, looking desperately for Lou. Where the hell was she? I walked into a bush in the dark and bumped into Monsieur Paëlla who had unexpectedly replaced my hot rabbit of a brother-in-law in the arms of Anna Pavlovna. *Pauvre Laurent.* I sympathized. After all he had done to foster Franco-Bulgarian understanding. All those phone calls, all that melodrama, all that under-wear – to lose the woman of your dreams to a spicy caterer! Life was unjust. I found him sobbing in Gisèle's arms as she stroked his head. The single malt had done the trick. She had spilled the beans, told him all about Dylan and his canary cannabis seed.

'He is so upset. *Tellement navré,*' she whispered to me. '*Regarde la détresse d'un père.*'

Laurent's tears were not for Dylan, but she clasped him to her forgiving bosom, savouring the moment. Lucky Laurent. I'd need a quick clasp myself soon if I didn't find Lou. Suddenly, there was the sound of exploding fireworks. I froze. Gunpowder excited Ariane's libido. I must act quickly before she caught up with me!

Someone told me they had seen Lou going down towards the car park. I was seized with a terrible pre-monition, the Cassandra within me awoken by these words. Who was she going to see in the car park? Why wasn't she looking for me? I shoved my way through the throng, busily knocking back plastic beakers of sangria, bumping into a gut that made the noise of a Hollofil pillow – doubtless a Weight Watcher – guided by a cosmic intuition. I knew what was happening. I knew it in my bones.

I ran down the steep lane leading to the Porte Royale, hanging on to the ivy on the walls to keep my balance,

turned the corner and was stopped dead in my tracks by
a vision of horror.

There before me, in the warm dark of the *nuit
lochoise*, silhouetted against the appallingly vulgar tank,
were Lou and Mortier. Their conversation was intense.
They were unaware of my presence, of my pained,
staccato breathing in the dark behind them. What had
they got to say to each other? What was going on? Why
this need to be alone, to flee the throng, to hide in the
car park? And then it happened. The gods, seated on
a dark cloud overlooking Loches, gave the optician
a nudge. *Just do it, Gérard.* And he, filled with evil
purpose, did it. He put his hand behind Lou's neck,
pulled her face towards his and kissed her.

Il l'a embrassée. Le salaud!

Lights flashed on and off. The car horn sirened into
the night. The vibrations of my pain had set off the
alarm.

My world collapsed.

C'en est trop. It was too much.

I fled, alone, back into the night.

23

Oui. Trop c'est trop. When it comes to emotions, we Brits can show the Latins what it means to be volcanic. I decided to pack and leave there and then. On an impulse. What was the point in hanging around. France had decided to say no to England? Too bad. *Tant pis.* I had done my best. I had squirted my turret, chosen my moment, prepared my text. In vain. Tragedy is like that. The just are punished unjustly. Filled with anger and spite, I tossed my shirts into a suitcase. To be dumped for an opulent optician – *quelle honte.* People would point me out in the street. I would be unable to raise my head again.

I emptied the dishwasher, closed the shutters and locked the door behind me. The leeks, panicking, clamoured from the bottom of the garden.

'Maï-quel!' they implored. 'Please don't leave us like this! A word, a hug before you go!'

But I was resolute, deaf to the cries of my orphan vegetables. The Mazda roared angrily into life.

Adieu, Toison. Farewell, the Toison d'Or with its battered Miko ice-cream sign. Ciao forever to Pois-Chiche and his municipal flowerbed. The headlights for the last time picked out a dusty Father Christmas, cooked by the summer sun, endlessly endeavouring to climb into Henri's bedroom with his sack full of silver-wrapped gifts. Never again would I see the chorus of moustached ladies in their orange crash helmets waiting for the frozen food lorry. Salut, Père Jules. Give the rabbits a kiss from me. I'll send you a postcard from Dover.

I drove through Mouzay, past the garage of Marcellin, my brother in woe. Marcellin had adopted the only solution possible to conceal his ill-timed declaration. On the wall of the garage were now seven big yellow letters. R-E-N-A-U-L-T. What did this mean? That Marcellin, having dumped Citroën, had decided to accept another franchise? The answer was simple. The new contract was the only way to conceal his desperate cry of love. The 'N' was perfectly placed.

R - E - N - A - U - L - T
M - O - N - I - Q - U - E
The make of a car now hid the mark of love.

Such is the lot of unrequited passion. Just stop to peer behind the shop signs of *la France profonde*. Put your nose to the wall and look up, and under the flashing neon of Proxi, Mini-Marché, Panier fleuri, you'll discover the long-faded paintwork of the declarations of lovesick *commerçants*. Angèle! Marcelle! Monique!

I drove north fast and hard. On the screen of my mind I endlessly and perversely replayed the scene I had most not wanted to see. *Ext. Night.* Loches. Two silhouettes against a black tank. The camera moves in on them. He raises his hands. He pulls her face towards his. His libidinous optician's eyes devour her. He kisses her. Passionately. He groans, *'Oublie-le rosbif!'*

And she, hoarse with desire, answers, *'Mords-moi, Gérard.'*

The scene is terrible. The dialogue shit. This is no way to end. She can't spend the rest of her life polishing his Quad! Not the heroine! Call that a climax? The story can't stop there!

I was seized with an appalling thought. Was this to be the conclusion of my *éducation sentimentale*? Edith Delluc volume one, Ariane Tricot volume two, Lou Charpin, volume three. The Failure Trilogy.

I drove on north towards the sea. At four o'oclock in the morning I found myself parked on the central square of Mortagne, the world capital of *boudin*. It was a bitter reminder. In the courtyard of Aimé's farm I should never have hesitated. I had a bootful of *boudin*? I should have seized the moment. *There is a tide in the affairs of men which, taken at the flood* . . .

Sitting down wearily on a bench, I surveyed the devastated landscape of my future. I was not, after all, to belong to my own French family. I was never to have my place at table, my checked napkin in a drawer, my ritual glass of Ambassadeur as I sat down to a lethal game of Scrabble. Never again would I climb on a stool to inspect the St-Maure goat's cheese, never again would I receive my Christmas gift wrapped in an aluminium freezer tray. Goodbye, *andouillettes* and constipation, farewell canaries and cannabis. The curtain was rapidly falling, the vibrant present dissolving into an insipid future.

How beautiful France was in the depths of the night. I was bewitched by the charms of Mortagne. I am going to miss you, Crédit Agricole, with your flashing all-night cash machine. I don't want to leave you behind, *Mod's Hair, salon de coiffure mixte conseil styliste*. Soon dawn would break, and beaten-up small lorries would arrive with their crates of crisp, dew-drenched lettuces. Old wizened ladies would begin to display a *cageot* of new potatoes with their wonderful names –

des rattes, des cornes de bique – a few duck eggs, a *fromage frais* on a rickety table. But when they do, I shall be gone, back to the world of Tesco and freezer packs.

Suddenly, sitting on my nocturnal bench, I had a revelation. The solution for Emmeline's tombstone came in a flash. All she had to do was to get the mason to carve a marble Scrabble stand. And on it, in disarray, the letters spelling out her name: E-E-E-M-L-N-I. Visitors would stop, arrested by the novelty. And then inevitably, because 98 per cent of visitors to cemeteries play Scrabble, they would scratch their heads and begin to rearrange the letters. E-M-M-E-L-I-N-E. Counts double for eternity.

Brilliant. But too late.

On the outskirts of Rouen I spotted an all-night McDonald's. I was hungry and tired. Plastic on the walls, plastic on the floors, plastic in the bun. A taste of things to come. It was crazy to leave. I wanted check tablecloths, white aprons, red wine in bottles without labels, cheese that walked to the table by itself, coffee that kept you awake for a week. I held on tight to the France they were taking away from me.

And what would I do, once back in England? Where could I go? I'd told everyone I was getting married. I couldn't face up to failure. Not again. I'd have to move somewhere else, change my name, grow a moustache. I'd open a bed and breakfast in Bangor. Sit by the electric fire in a gravy-stained cardy, stroking the neck of my fat Labrador. *La vie est foutue.*

In what seemed no time I was in Dieppe. I loved Dieppe, but I loved it for arriving. Not for leaving. The Transmanche Ferry awaited at the quay like the large yellow coffin of my dreams and aspirations.

Before saying farewell, one last pleasure. Every-thing had begun, everything would end with a cheese. If I were to forget le colonel, life would not be worth living.

The cheese shop, *my* cheese shop, was slumbering in the shade of the cathedral. As I stepped inside, they were all there to greet me, as if they knew that this was my final bow. I was moved. They had come decked out in their finery to bid me farewell and I moved from one to the next, bidding them farewell in turn – the *tommes*, the *bûches*, the *pyramides*, the *pavés*, the *roues*, the *cendrés*, the *crottins*, the *crayeux*, the *bleus*, the *fourmes*, the *chevrotins*, the *boutons*. I had a word for the *morbiers*, and for the *chaources*, a joke for the *salers*, a hug for the *beauforts*. But they all knew that my heart was taken.

I had once two loves. Now only one remains.

'Un livarot, s'il-vous-plaît.'

Car elle est, ma préférence à moi.

The owner, himself at least 60 per cent *matière grasse*, oozed from the back of the shop, my cheese in his hand.

'Mais, il vous attendait, Monsieur Sadler.'

Attendait? An imperfect? *Was waiting.* And he knew my name?

'A lady phoned for you,' he went on.

For me? In a cheese shop?

'Il y a un Post-it.'

A note was attached to the box. My colonel had something to tell me. After Interflora, Intercheese.

Idiot, said the note. *Tu ne comprends donc rien?*

Was it possible I had misunderstood that awful kiss? The William Tell overture rang painfully in my ears.

C'était un baiser d'adieu, the message went on. A farewell kiss. A parting gift.

Reviens vite. Je t'aime. Lou.

I read the Post-it twenty-three times. I then recited it to the choir of cheeses who dried a tear and applauded.

Elle m'aime. Lou m'aime. It was there, written in words of fire on the Livarot box.

I stepped outside. The people of Dieppe had gathered around the shop in anticipation. As I emerged, they started to sing and to dance like the chorus in a film by Jacques Demy. A band of angels descended from the sky, landed in the cathedral car park and joined in.

Dazed, I went down on to the pebbly beach. In the distance, a lady in pink kept a careful eye on her paddling spaniel. The wind was from the south. I knew it would carry my words. I stood, slightly formal and erect on the beach and looked out across the Channel in order to address the ghosts of my parents waiting for the news on the beach at Newhaven.

'Mum, Dad. *Je reste.* Things are fine. *Ça baigne.* All is well. *Je vous embrasse.*'

And then euphoria took hold of me. Alone on the beach, I started to dance. A *pas de deux.* For an Englishman and his cheese. *Duo pour rosbif et livarot.*

It was time to return.

On m'attend à la maison.